GIVIN' IT
THEIR ALL

GIVIN' IT THEIR ALL

The Backstreet Boys' Rise to the Top

Sherri Rifkin

BALLANTINE BOOKS • NEW YORK

This is an independent biographical work and is not authorized by the Backstreet Boys.

A Ballantine Book
Published by The Ballantine Publishing Group
Copyright © 1998 by Sherri Rifkin
Astrological Profiles copyright © 1998 by Andrea Valeria

Cover photo © Melanie Edwards/Retna

http://www.randomhouse.com

Library of Congress Catalog Card Number: 98-96117

ISBN 0-345-42654-1

Printed in Canada

First Edition: August 1998

10   9   8   7

Contents

Acknowledgments

A *big* thanks to the members of my own posse, who were instrumental in making this recording session possible:

My A&R directors, JAG.C and Robbie-Rob, for their ongoing support from the West Coast office; DJ Jon G., for providing the audio portion; my favorite Flavor, Vanilla, for harmonizing with me and keeping me cheerful through the creative process; my producer, Mattie S., for providing the video portion in exchange for some raw fish and random dinner companions; my BB homegirls, LMH and ERZ (who is also my master mixer), for continuing the circle; my Canadian correspondent, Jessica H., for writing some of the "lyrics"; sistas Rachel C. and Sarah C., my London correspondents, for their fantastic words, and their cool cuz, Alby, for hooking us up; my mystical advisor, Andrea V., for translating the message from the skies; my favorite rock critic, Bob M., for adding his salient observations; my "agent," Anne E., for making sure everything is kosher; and the crew at Ballantine who edited, mixed, mastered,

engineered, and manufactured this track quickly to
meet market demands.

Special props go to the original Hester Street Boy, Rif
Daddy, for just about everything else.

Meet the Boys!

The fans have been waiting outside the hall for hours, maybe even since the night before. They are with their best friends, and perhaps with a parent or older sibling who has come along to make sure everything goes okay. They have been anticipating this night for weeks. Maybe they already stood in line outside this very hall for tickets weeks before. Maybe they dialed the telephone number for the ticket agency over and over again until they finally got through. Maybe they won the tickets in a local radio station contest. No matter how they got the tickets, the fact is that they *have* these precious pieces of paper in their hands, and they are not letting them go until they must hand them to the ticket-taker, who will finally allow them into the hall.

At last the gates open and the girls—thousands of them—are allowed in. The crowd surges forward once the buzz moves back to the farther reaches of the line that the time has come for these dedicated fans to be let in at last. After all, haven't they been waiting forever? It seems that way.

Their tickets are ripped in half, and the fans race

into the hall, cardboard signs, teddy bears, roses, and chaperones in tow. The wide-open space that was empty and silent just moments before now fills with thousands of people within minutes. The fans settle themselves in the best spot they can find, which with some luck has a decent view of the stage. The stage is set fairly high up, so even though thousands of people will be standing at the same level, they should be able to see well enough. But even though they have now staked out their positions, they must wait some more. It seems like an eternity.

The noise in the hall increases as the thousands of people pour in. Soon chanting begins: "Back-street Boys. Back-street Boys." It starts softly, swells, reaches an ear-shattering, floor-stomping pitch, and then subsides again. It starts again a few minutes later, washing over the crowd in waves. Some people are singing snippets of songs. Others are climbing up on their friends' shoulders to get a better view of the stage and find out what is going on, but the only thing they see is roadies walking back and forth across the stage, moving equipment around, seemingly meaninglessly. When will they leave the stage so the show can begin?

Finally the lights go down and the screaming starts. The fans don't even realize how loud they are; because they are so happy and excited, the screams and yells of delight just come out of their mouths spontaneously. The chanting begins again, only much louder than before. It continues nonstop for several minutes, people stamping their feet to keep the beat. They wave their signs high in the air and hold up sparklers and lighters, trying to will the Boys onto the stage. Spotlights start to pan over the crowd, momentarily lighting up the thousands of hands waving in the air, alternating between bathing them in bright white light and plunging them into darkness.

The spotlights go out and a momentary hush falls over the crowd as the tiniest bit of music is heard. Ten, maybe twenty seconds of the song "Everybody (Backstreet's Back)," and then silence. A pause. More screaming.

At last a man's deep voice is heard over the loudspeaker—a thunderous noise, even louder than the chanting. "Good evening, ladies and gentlemen! Welcome to [whatever hall, stadium, forum, or center]! We have a very special show for you tonight!" Suddenly two huge screens above the stage light up, flashing larger-than-life baby and childhood pictures of the Boys as the announcer says the following: "And now we present A.J. . . . Kevin . . . B-Rok . . . Howie D. . . . and Nick! Ladies and gentlemen . . . *the Backstreet Boys*!"

Screams of joy fill the hall. It's deafening. It rocks the house. It feels as if the concrete is moving beneath their feet. Darkness again.

Then the voice returns with a countdown: "Ten, nine, eight, seven, six, five, four, three, two . . . *one*!" The stage lights up and suddenly there they are—the Backstreet Boys—striking poses, wearing various red, white, and blue nylon racing outfits. They move around the stage, waving hello to their joyous fans, the smiles on the Boys' faces matching those of their audience. They sing a snippet of the childhood favorite "If You're Happy And You Know It," and the fans scream back in response. Then the Boys start doing a short introductory rap. The audience goes wild.

The band starts almost out of nowhere, and the Boys launch into their first song, appropriately "Let's Have A Party," with Nick singing lead. This show—and the hundreds of others that the Backstreet Boys have performed in their more than three-year career—is nothing less than a fabulous party. They are onstage for more than an hour, singing, harmonizing, dancing, smiling, waving, serenading, *connecting*—and the fans couldn't love them more for it.

No matter what country they are in, no matter how many consecutive days they have been on the road and away from their homes and families, no matter how many times they have sung "Boys Will Be Boys" or "As Long As You Love Me" over and over again, no matter how many times they have heard the delighted screams of their adoring fans, the Boys always give it their all. And never, ever anything less.

It's no mystery, really, that the Backstreet Boys are a huge national and international megagroup, adored equally by fans in Singapore and San Francisco, in New Zealand and New York. The Backstreet Boys have a great sound; beautiful, sweet, smooth-as-silk harmonies; slamming dance moves; catchy songs, both slow and fast; handsome faces; positive outlooks; and, not the least of it, a genuine appreciation for their fans. It's a love fest between fans all over the world and these regular, down-to-earth guys home-grown in Florida and Kentucky. Who can resist this charming fivesome when they answer that they will stay together and sing for their fans "As Long As You Love Me"?

For many American fans, it seems as if the Backstreet Boys came out of nowhere when they started burning up the charts in the summer of 1997. But the Boys first came together in 1993 and became a major international sensation in as many as thirty-five countries starting in 1995 before returning to the United States to conquer their home turf. Theirs is a Cinderella story of sorts, especially since the Boys first got their start not far from (and maybe partially because of?) the Magic Kingdom itself.

Ironically, the Boys have a self-admitted reputation as being the world's most popular group no one has ever heard of. But mention the song "Quit Playing Games (With My Heart)" and people of all ages will start singing this smash single—"na, na, na, na, na's" and all.

In this book you will get up close and personal with each of these five funky guys: A.J. McLean, Nick Carter, Brian "B-Rok" Littrell, Kevin "Kev" Richardson, and Howie "Howie D." Dorough. You will get the inside scoop on everything from their loves to their dislikes, their individual talents, their childhoods, their secrets, their dreams, and their hopes for the future. You will find out how the Boys first came together and why, where their interest in music came from, how they followed their dreams without looking back, and how they made it to the top of the national and international music scene (beautiful voices, talent, and smokin' good looks never hurt!). We'll follow the Boys' rise to international stardom (it took a lot of hard work and many nights sleeping on cold tour buses) and tell how and why the group conquered foreign lands before they returned to the good ol' U.S. of A.

Follow the Boys on their adventures all over the world. Meet some of the most dedicated BSB fans (a few of whom have written personal accounts in this book just for you). Find out to what lengths some daring fans will go to get a face-to-face with their favorite Boys. Get an exclusive look at what it is like backstage before the show. Check out the chapter about the Boys' original sense of style, both as a group and individually. Get the scoop on each of the guys' love life sitches: whether or not they are currently involved, what they would do on a dream date, who is the most romantic of the five, and who has had a touch of not-so-great luck in love (you might be surprised).

While I didn't actually meet the Boys or interview them for this book, I did do lots of research on the Boys from several U.S. and international sources—including fan magazines, Web sites, and newspapers—to give you, the dedicated BSB fan, the best all-out scoop I could. It's all about helping you keep the Backstreet pride alive.

Now, on with the show!

PART ONE

The Real Story Behind the Backstreet Boys

CHAPTER 1

Coming Together

Flashback to early 1993. The place is Orlando, Florida. No one knows who the Backstreet Boys are (can you imagine such a time?), because they haven't all met one another and the group does not yet exist. At this point, the five future members—A.J. McLean, Howie Dorough, Nick Carter, Kevin Richardson, and Brian Littrell—are only cosmically connected in one way or another. Though they are aware of their own personal dreams, hopes, and desires, they don't yet know that soon they will be members of what will become, in just a couple of years, one of the hottest music groups in the world.

Magical Beginnings

In a way, you could think of Disney World and its environs as the birthplace of the Backstreet Boys. The Magic Kingdom certainly worked its own brand of magic on the lives of five boys, all of whom shared the dream of singing, dancing, and performing for others—*thousands* of others. Disney World was like a magnet, drawing the boys together in one place and changing their lives forever.

So how'd they all get there?

A.J., Howie, and Nick were the first to meet one another. The three of them all lived in the Orlando, Florida, area at the time. A.J. and Howie coincidentally (or fatefully, depending on how you look at it) shared the same vocal coach. The voice coach introduced them, probably because these two boys were about the same age, had similar sounds, and liked the same kind of music.

The three guys were also individually making the rounds of local auditions at places such as Universal and MGM Studios, so they would often run into one another there. They started to talk and pass the time together while waiting their turn to be called. It was then that these three realized that they had a lot in common—namely, music. They shared similar tastes in the artists and style of music they liked to listen to and sing.

So one day while they were hanging out, they decided to try singing something together. They harmonized to a song by the Temptations. They really liked the way their voices sounded together and thought, "Hey, why not form an a cappella singing group?" (*A cappella* means "without instrumental accompaniment.")

Kevin Richardson had recently made his way south to work in Disney World. In 1991 he was living at home in Lexington, Kentucky, dreaming about getting into big-time entertainment. Growing up, he had loved all kinds of music and had sung in church choirs. After graduating from high school, he had moved on to doing some singing with a local Top 40 cover band, but that wasn't satisfying him, so he started making plans for something bigger and better. Luckily, Kevin didn't have to stray too far from home to check out showbiz. Because a lot of television and movie work was starting to become available in Orlando, Florida, at that time, Kevin didn't have to relocate to New York City or Los Angeles to try making a go of his dream.

He packed up his bags and headed to Orlando to see what kind of work he could find there. The first gig he got was as a tour guide at Disney World. It was a beginning, that's for sure. What also made him happy was that the job allowed him some time to practice his singing and do some songwriting. He then landed parts at Disney as a Teenage Mutant Ninja Turtle and Aladdin (a character who had a lot of magic on his side).

Not too long after Kevin got settled, a friend of his heard him singing and thought he had a great voice. The friend asked Kevin if he wanted to try singing with some other guys he knew who had formed an a cappella group. Guess which group that was? Yup—A.J., Howie, and Nick's group. The trio met Kevin and dug the way his voice blended with their sound, so they asked him to join up.

Then came a big opportunity. The guys saw an advertisement in the local newspaper looking for those who were interested in forming a boy band. The ad was placed by Louis J. Pearlman, who was not only the cousin of Art Garfunkel (one half of Simon and Garfunkel, a famous singing duo from the '60s and '70s) but also was starting a record company.

Before deciding to get into the music biz, Lou Pearlman had been the owner of a very profitable company in Orlando called Airship International Ltd., which provided the blimps that flew ads for big corporations like Budweiser and McDonald's high over sports stadiums and other outdoor events. But in the 1970s Louis had been a musician in his own right: He played guitar in a band in New York that actually was the opener for well-known artists of the time, such as Barry White and Gloria Gaynor. So by the early 1990s he was ready to return to the music world, but this time to help other young artists get their start.

Louis Pearlman hired two talent agents in Florida, Scott Hoekstra and Jeanne Tanzy, to hold auditions for performers interested in forming a "boy band." The talent agents put an ad in the local papers and set up auditions for fifty hopeful candidates, four of which were none other than A.J. McLean, Nick Carter, Howie Dorough, and Kevin Richardson.

The four guys nailed the audition, but all thought they needed a fifth to round out their sound. Kevin had the good idea of calling his cousin Brian Littrell back home in Kentucky and convincing him to come down to audition as well. Kevin and Brian had grown up together and were very close, especially because they shared a musical bond. When they were younger, both sang in choirs at local churches. They also had grown up entertaining their large extended family by singing doo-wop, barbershop quartet music, and their favorite contemporary songs. As Brian got older, he especially started to like the smooth sounds of R&B, counting Luther Vandross as one of his influences.

The story goes that Brian was in history class when he heard his name being announced on the school loudspeaker. At first he was worried that it was bad news, but when he left class, got on the phone, and heard his cousin Kevin's excited voice telling him to come down to Florida immediately, Brian knew fate was at work somehow. Fully aware of the once-in-a-lifetime opportunity his cousin described to him, Brian got his act together very quickly and hightailed it to Orlando by plane the very next day to audition in the hopes of becoming the fifth member. The combo of their five voices worked like—you guessed it—*magic*. A group was born.

Once the five guys joined up, they needed a name—something catchy, yet something that told where they came from. In Orlando there was a flea market called the Backstreet Market, which was the center of a lot of activity. When the market was not set up, the space was a big, empty parking lot, so the kids in the area appropriated it as their local hangout. They would drive up in their cars, socialize, and listen to music. So the group adopted the name "Backstreet." They added on "Boys" because, as Kevin once explained in a radio interview overseas, "No matter how old we get, we'll always be Boys. And back in the U.S., when you say we're 'Boys,' that means that you are friends." So the name "Backstreet Boys" was created! Unfortunately, the actual market no longer exists, because a new building has been built on the lot. But its memory will live on in the name the Boys chose for themselves.

Getting Down to Work

The newly formed Backstreet Boys were enthusiastic from the start. They were thrilled to be working together and knew they had a good thing going, so they dedicated themselves to making big things happen for the five of them. They knew this was their chance, so they pulled together as a team, and soon began feeling like a family. They learned to rely on their instincts, their experience in entertainment, and their talents. But first they needed to get used to working with one another and get their act down.

They began by rehearsing at Louis Pearlman's warehouse in Kissimmee, singing covers of hits by contemporary artists, such as Boyz II Men's "It's So Hard To Say Goodbye To Yesterday" and Shai's "If I Ever Fall In Love" (which BSB still sings live to this day), as well as tunes by veteran artists such as Smokey Robinson. To practice, get more comfortable performing live, and start making new fans, the Boys spent a lot of time doing gigs at high schools, theme parks like Sea World, and talent shows in the Orlando, Florida, area.

They also auditioned wherever they needed to—restaurants, boardrooms, office lobbies—in front of everyone from the press to high-flying record execs at major music labels looking to sign the next hot thing. Those people who saw them in the early days were ready to compare the Boys to one of their successful predecessors, New Kids on the Block. However, it was clear that these Boys had a special quality to them and a natural talent that could possibly make them even bigger stars than NKOTB, which was popular in the 1980s.

As the Boys got used to each other and learned their individual strong points, they started to add in their unique brand of funk and original BSB flavor. They knew they did amazing harmonies together but wanted to add their own personalities and style to the mix. And since all five Boys knew how to move to the groove, they added some slick dance routines to their act, and BSB was on their way.

Soon the Boys were ready to record their very first single. It was a track called "Tell Me That I'm Dreaming," which was a song that Lou Pearlman himself had composed. BSB recorded this single for Pearlman's independent record label, called Trans Continental. Pearlman then made hundreds of copies of the song on cassette so they could hand them out not only to fans at the Boys' early appearances and shows but also to record-business people to get the word out about the new Boys.

It was clear that Lou really believed in the Boys from the very beginning and had only the highest of hopes for them. In a 1993 article about him in the *Orlando Sentinel*, Lou said he was already thinking about the day when BSB would come back home to be the headlining performers at the Orlando Arena. In the liner notes of the Boys' U.S.-released self-titled CD that came out four years after they first got together,

A.J. thanks Lou, a.k.a. "Big Poppa," and calls him "our brother, father, friend, and the list goes on."

In July 1993 Pearlman asked the music management team of Donna and Johnny Wright, of Wright Stuff Management, to come on board to work with the Boys. Pearlman approached Donna and her husband, Johnny, because they had been the management team behind the whopping success of New Kids on the Block (Johnny was their tour manager).

While Pearlman was high on the Wrights, at first the husband-wife team wasn't sure if they wanted to take on another boy band—even though they had done so well with NKOTB and clearly knew the market for this genre of music. The Wrights were finally convinced to work with BSB by first seeing a videotape of the Boys performing at Grad Nite at Sea World in May '93 and then hearing them sing a cappella live at a local restaurant. After hearing their harmonies, Donna Wright saw that these five guys had some major talent and that the group would have wide appeal outside of their hometown. It also helped that most of the Boys already had some experience working professionally in the entertainment business. She told the *Los Angeles Times*, "When I first heard the Backstreet Boys, I got the chills so strong that the hairs stood up straight on the back of my neck."

Right out of the gate, the Wrights started working their connections to get BSB some major attention and performing experience. The Wrights arranged for the Backstreet Boys to open for After 7 and Young MC at a concert in Portland, Oregon, at the Civic Arena. In the fall of 1993 BSB then did a national tour of high schools, ending with stops at schools in central Florida in October. BSB also began forming a solid fan base by performing at junior high and high schools and other small venues, like theme parks and summer festivals, where the audiences were mostly kids. Doing these smaller gigs also gave the Boys time to polish and perfect their act by getting live feedback from their audiences.

Because the Boys promoted clean living, no drugs, and other positive messages and came from fairly religious upbringings, other kids immediately related to the Boys and their music. What also helped win over new fans was that from the start, BSB always made it a priority to meet and be accessible to as many people in their audience as they could, which is something they continue to do to this day, even after becoming a huge success. In the early days, getting up close and personal with the people who cheered them on and supported them helped BSB lay a solid groundwork for the future.

While all of this was totally exciting for the BSB crew, by no means was this time in their lives all fun and games. Performing as a new group for audiences who had never heard them was a nerve-wracking experience for the fivesome. They were passionate about proving that they were not just another group of handsome faces with one kind of sound—or worse, a fake sound. Since they could naturally sing and harmonize beautifully together, they wanted to set themselves apart from the music acts that came before them, including the New Kids on the Block. They

were determined to get out from under that shadow
and create their own sound and look—and they
worked to make that happen.

Once the Boys got more experience under their
belts, the Wrights then started setting up bigger gigs
for the group: opening for major, solid acts that drew
audiences of all ages, such as Richard Marx, Kenny G,
REO Speedwagon, and the Village People. BSB also
started performing at music festivals in different parts
of the United States to expand the group's exposure.
The plan worked like a charm. Soon the Boys were
opening for major acts who were performing locally,
such as Brandy, Jon Secada, and En Vogue.

The Big Break

Since they were doing an awesome job at their live
performances, the Boys, Lou Pearlman, and the
Wrights thought that BSB was ready to go after a
recording deal with a major label. Luckily, Donna had
some strong connections in the music biz from her
days of working with NKOTB. For a while she had
been urging her friend David McPherson, who was
then a talent scout at Mercury Records in New York,
to listen to the new group she was working with. So
one day while the Boys were up onstage performing
in a concert in Cleveland, she called McPherson
on her cellular phone, held it up high, and let the
Boys' sweet voices—and the fans' enthusiastic cheers
and screams—speak for themselves. As it turns out,

McPherson wasn't home, but his answering machine recorded the wild reaction of the crowd. When he heard the message, he was so intrigued that he decided to meet the Boys at their next stop. After seeing what all the hype was about firsthand, McPherson immediately saw that the Backstreet Boys had what it took to be a big sensation. So the Boys signed a recording contract with Mercury Records in 1993.

Soon after, McPherson left Mercury to become an A&R director at Jive Records, an R&B label. Probably since the time for BSB's unique brand of pop music wasn't yet right (see Chapter 3 for some background info), Mercury dropped BSB without ever doing anything with them. So McPherson, knowing what kind of potential the five guys from Florida had goin' on, signed the band to Jive Records. The Boys were pumped about going with Jive, since R. Kelly, who is one of the Boys' idols, was also signed to Jive. And it didn't take long for the Backstreet Boys and Jive Records to become a winning combo.

From the very beginning, Dave jumped in to work with the Boys. His first order of business: help them refine their act, sign up some of the best music producers in the industry to work with them, and get them into the studio to start recording ASAP.

While each of the Boys had natural talent and basic performing skills, McPherson saw that they still needed to polish up their singing and dancing abilities so that they would be in top form to record and tour. The Boys were more than ready for the challenge, and they were able to take advantage of all kinds of valuable resources that were now available to them through working with a major record label. So the Boys started collaborating with professional vocal coaches, stylists, choreographers, producers, and musicians who could help bring them to the next level.

The sound BSB was going for was an original mix of R&B, hip-hop, blues, gospel, and pop. Vocal harmony needed to be a big part of whatever they did. To get inspiration, they looked to a wide variety of artists. First they studied the music they had listened to while they were growing up, such as Manhattan Transfer, the Temptations, the Four Tops, and the Stylistics. The more contemporary sounds they really loved and wanted to draw from were Boyz II Men, Jodeci, Shai, New Edition, Jon Secada, Bobby Brown, Steve Perry from Journey, and Color Me Badd.

At last, in 1995, they were ready to roll—into the studio to record their first single for Jive. The Boys got on a plane to go to Stockholm, Sweden, to work with Denniz PoP of Ace of Base fame. Denniz produced the group's first single, "We've Got It Goin' On," which the Backstreet Boys recorded in his studio, called Cheiron Studios.

With the release of this single, the Backstreet Boys would soon learn that they really did have it goin' on.

CHAPTER 2

Conquering the World

By early 1995 the Backstreet Boys were ready to release their first single under the Jive Records label. The Boys had flown to Sweden to record "We've Got It Goin' On" with the help of Ace of Base's Denniz PoP. The single was released simultaneously in both the United States and Europe. The American music scene being what it was in 1995—that is, still heavily into grunge and harder-edged music—the single only made it to the number sixty-nine position on *Billboard* magazine's Hot 100 chart. For many reasons, the States weren't ready for the silky-smooth sounds of the Backstreet Boys. (Chapter 3 gives the full scoop.)

Taking It Across the Ocean

But magic was still on the Boys' side. The single fared much better in both the United Kingdom and Germany, where boy bands like Take That and Boyzone were topping the charts. "We've Got It Goin' On" went into heavy rotation on English radio stations, giving Brits their first listen to the newest act from America. *Smash Hits* magazine in England gave the single a five-star review. So by the time the group held an official and exclusive launch party for the single at Planet Hollywood in London, the English press had worked itself into a frenzy about this new pop sensation from across the ocean.

The Boys started making the first of several appearances on British TV. They appeared on the Brit variety program called *Live and Kicking* the Saturday after the party and blew everyone away with their style, energy, and most of all their music. Not too much later, the Boys were invited to make an appearance on *Top of the Pops*, a popular music show in England. In the summer of 1995 the Boys hit the road, touring Europe with Duncan and P.J., which gave the Boys great exposure to new fans on the Continent. The group then joined Ant and Dec's Christmas Cracker Tour, sealing their popularity with their new English fans. Audiences all over the U.K. and Europe had become smitten by the fresh-faced Boys from Florida.

Kevin provided some insight about the group's almost instant success in the U.K. in a 1997 article in the *Orlando Sentinel*: "At the time, there were a lot of what they called 'boy bands' over there. But they saw that we were more than just pretty faces. When we started singing a cappella, they were like, 'Oh, they're for real.' "

The second single the Boys released was "I'll Never Break Your Heart." This song, though a slower, ballad-type love song, unlike the faster, danceable first single, climbed the English charts to become the group's second hit. An early sign of critical success for BSB came at the *Smash Hits* Awards show in England, during which the Backstreet Boys claimed the prize for Best New Tour Act of 1995.

German fans were quick to jump on the BSB bandwagon, too. The single "I'll Never Break Your Heart" went gold in Germany and became the number one hit in Austria. In 1996 the viewers of VIVA, a German music TV channel, voted BSB the number one boy band.

Canada—though across a very wide ocean from the U.K. and Europe—was not far behind in terms of catching on to the BSB sensation, and by February 1996 the single and its video were in heavy rotation on both radio stations and music video channels in Montreal. Kevin told *Billboard* magazine about how quickly BSB became popular with Canadian fans between the group's first visit to Quebec, which was in February 1996—before BSB even released their CD there—and their return some months later. In February the Boys were scheduled to do a basically routine appearance at a mall in Montreal called Place Vertu. Even then, three thousand fans showed up to see them perform, which, considering how early it was in their career, was a great turnout. By the time the Backstreet Boys returned to the Montreal area to perform at the Festival des Montgolfières in St.-Jean-sur-Richelieu in August of that same year, they had an audience of sixty-five thousand people! The Boys were more blown away by this than the fans were!

What is truly magical and wonderful about BSB's early success is that not only was all this happening for them less than a year after they released their first single, but they hadn't even released an album yet! By 1996 fans in most of Europe and Canada were now anxiously waiting for the Boys to release a full-length CD, but they would have to wait patiently for a few more months for their request to be filled.

Then something quite dramatic and fateful happened: In early 1996 the beloved English group Take That, probably BSB's foremost competitor, split up, sending millions of fans into hysteria. It was an unfortunate turn for those who loved Take That, but the group's breakup allowed more room for the Backstreet Boys to move onto the music scene abroad and up the charts—into the hearts of the mourning fans. (Again, you'll find more info about this story in Chapter 3.)

At last, in April 1996, the group released their much-anticipated debut international album, the self-titled *Backstreet Boys*. Along with it, they released their third single, called "Get Down (You're The One For Me)." Both the single and the CD soared to the top of the charts. They immediately earned an award for Best Newcomers at London's Red Nose Awards in May 1996.

The fans, however, were not completely satisfied yet. They wanted their Boys to tour so they could see their sexy dance moves and hear their melodious voices *live*. And the Boys, never ones to disappoint their loyal fans, came through in the biggest way!

The Backstreet Boys set out on a tour throughout Europe and the United Kingdom in the summer of 1996. This was the first tour on which the Boys were the top act, which must have made them a little nervous at first. But they had nothing to worry about: They sold out the tickets for all fifty-seven shows!

August marked the rerelease of the single "We've Got It Goin' On"—this time celebrated by another blowout bash at the Emporium, a posh London nightclub. Putting out the single for the second time sent it soaring to the top of the charts, since now this part of the world had caught on to BSB.

Backstreet Moves Forward—
And Across, Up, and Down Under

The tidal wave that was the Backstreet Boys also crashed onto the shores of Asia. When their self-titled CD was released there in September 1996, it blew out of the stores in Southeast Asia and sold more than six hundred thousand units in only ten weeks. It was love at first sight for the Asian fans. Their avid attention and admiration for the fivesome prompted a promotional tour through Asia, during which the Boys made their first stops in Singapore, Malaysia, and the Philippines. Their sellout tour included places like Hong Kong, Korea, Japan, Australia, New Zealand, and Malaysia.

At the same time, the Boys were scooping up awards left and right. In Germany they received the Best Newcomers Award at the VIVA Comet Awards. But the biggest coup of them all was beating out such megagroups as Oasis and the Spice Girls for the *Select* Award at the MTV Europe Awards in November 1996 in London, England. The *Select* Award is the equivalent of the MTV Viewer's Choice Award in the States. It is chosen by viewers of MTV Europe, who call in to request videos on the show called *Select*. Appropriately, Robbie Williams, who had just left Take That, presented BSB with the award that night. It was like he was passing on the crown to the new kings of pop. The Boys were overwhelmed with joy and emotion (some of the Boys even cried with happiness). They hadn't expected their success to come so quickly, especially when they were up against so many popular acts.

Then, in November 1996, it was time to release their fourth smash single, "Quit Playing Games (With My Heart)," and soon after, they embarked on their second megahuge tour of Europe. This time they hit countries such as Austria, Norway, Sweden, and France. In one year alone, the Boys appeared five times on *Top of the Pops* in England.

As a special Valentine's Day present for their loyal fans in Europe, the group released a special edition of "Anywhere For You" for February 1997, which included special V-Day messages from the Boys themselves. This personalized gift helped the single debut at the number four spot on the U.K. charts, while "Quit Playing Games" hit the Perfect Ten chart.

Meanwhile, in Canada, BSB mania was taking off. The frenzy started when their CD was released there in October 1996. By December 1996 BSB had sold 200,000 copies of their debut CD in Canada, 160,000 of which were sold in the French-speaking province of

Quebec. Montreal fans were among the most ardent, proving their BSB loyalty by scooping up the tickets for their January 3, 1997, show at the Molson Centre in just thirty minutes!

In Montreal, their vid for "We've Got It Goin' On" was the top clip on Plus TV—until their own video for "Get Down" beat it! Canadian fans even sent *The Backstreet Boys Home Video* to diamond status, meaning ten times platinum.

Since the Canadian fans were showing their Backstreet pride, the Boys made sure to bring their tour through Canada, with thirty-two stops in Quebec, Ontario, Manitoba, and British Columbia. This too proved to be an amazing sellout tour. Unbelievably, tickets to these concerts were so sizzling hot that they sold out in less than twenty minutes! All in all, seventy thousand fans saw the Boys perform live on their Canadian tour. And by April 1997 their self-titled CD had soared to the number one position on the charts and had gone platinum *six* times, selling six hundred thousand copies. The numbers were staggering.

No matter where the Boys went, it seemed, screaming, adoring fans were there to cheer them on. In the beginning of April 1997, still some months before the CD would be released south of the Canadian border (a.k.a. the United States), the Boys hit Winnipeg for a concert and a promotional appearance. Their first stop of the day was at a store in a shopping mall, where five thousand heavy-breathing fans crowded in, just to catch a glimpse of one of the handsome fivesome. In the evening, they were still in good enough shape to perform for another five thousand people at the Winnipeg Convention Center. How was Brian feeling before the concert? Nervous. He admitted to a reporter from the *Vancouver Province* newspaper, "If you're not nervous, something's wrong. It means you're not doing your best. At the same time, it is a rush, just knowing people are so excited to see you." Perhaps the word *excited* was a bit of an under-statement, since at the time he said this—fifteen min-utes before the doors of the Convention Center even opened—a huge crowd of eager, screaming fans was waiting outside. Later that week the Backstreet Boys performed for a crowd of more than seven thousand people at GM Place.

Going for Two

In September 1997 the Backstreet Boys released their second international CD in Europe, appropriately titled *Backstreet's Back*. This follow-up album was an exciting mix of new tracks that the Boys had just released on their American debut CD, as well as some previously unreleased hits.

In true BSB style, the guys threw a blowout bash to celebrate the release of their new international CD. By using some fancy satellite hookup, the Boys in New York were able to talk to the press all over the world. At the same time, the BSBs were finally enjoying their long-overdue recognition in their native country: The single "Quit Playing Games (With My Heart)" was topping the charts in the States, which made the Boys very happy. (Chapter 4 raves all about BSB's homecoming.)

By this time, Spain was also wild about the Boys from Orlando. The Backstreet Boys' debut album had gone platinum four times in that country, reaching sales of four hundred thousand units. Then, when *Backstreet's Back* was released in September 1997, it entered the Spanish charts at the number one position and then went triple platinum in less than three months' time!

By now the Boys were enjoying success all over the world, and it was keeping them hopping. BSB mania was sweeping the charts in places as far off as New Zealand and Australia. In the fall of 1997 "As Long As You Love Me" went to the number one spot in New Zealand, after debuting at number two! At the same time, the single "Everybody (Backstreet's Back)" was also in the top twenty, while the second album, *Backstreet's Back,* was in the top five. Down under in Australia, the single "Everybody (Backstreet's Back)" reached the top five. "As Long As You Love Me" also hit the top twenty and roared up the charts very quickly there.

By the end of 1997 BSB had made its mark all over the world in countries large and small. Their second CD, *Backstreet's Back*, had gone sextuple platinum in the Philippines; quintuple platinum in Malaysia; triple platinum in Taiwan and Indonesia; double platinum in Singapore, Hong Kong, and Thailand; platinum in India; and gold in Japan, Australia, Israel, and Korea.

Raking in the Awards

While the excitement for BSB was growing in all of these far-off countries, the passion for them only increased in the United Kingdom, where BSB's career first took off. On November 6, 1997, the Backstreet Boys won the *Select* Award at the MTV Europe Music Awards for the second year in a row—no easy feat, considering the power of the competition: the Spice Girls, Puff Daddy, and Hanson! This award was particularly meaningful for the Boys because it was chosen by MTV Europe viewers. Plus, the Boys were the only artists to perform twice on the awards show, singing "As Long As You Love Me" and also closing the show with "Everybody (Backstreet's Back)." They also had the honor of presenting Jon Bon Jovi the award for Best Male Vocalist.

Then a few weeks later, on November 30, 1997, the Backstreet Boys proved yet again that they were the reigning kings of pop music in the United Kingdom. That was the day of the *Smash Hits* Awards, which was held in London. The scene: the London Arena, filled to capacity with ten thousand people. Millions more watched the event live on BBC-TV. The competition was stiff—the Boys were up against big-time performers such as the Spice Girls and Peter Andre. You can just imagine the tension in that room.

Happily, our young heroes ruled the night by grabbing not one or two of these prestigious awards, but *five* (as in Fab Five!) awards. And not any old lame award categories, but the *top* awards. Check it out:

The Backstreet Boys were awarded:

1. Best International Band
2. Best Album, for *Backstreet's Back*
3. Best Album Cover for *Backstreet's Back*
4. Best Video for "Everybody" (from *Backstreet's Back*)
5. Best Male Haircut: Nick Carter

What's even more amazing is that no other band or musical artist won as many awards as the Boys. The Spicy Fivesome (a.k.a. the Spice Girls) won Best Group, but were shamed with the Worst Single award for "Spice Up Your Life," a cut from their second CD.

Headlines in the U.K. press cheered the dethroning of the Spice Queens by the Boys at the *Smash Hits* Awards. The *Daily Express* declared that "the spectacular success of . . . the Backstreet Boys left Girl Power looking distinctly out of date." The *Daily Mail* commented that the audience went wildest with excitement for the Backstreet Boys' live performance of "Everybody." The *Sun* said that the Boys "stole the show."

The Great White North

The Backstreet Boys released their second album, *Backstreet's Back,* in Canada on August 12, 1997. By November 23 it had reached the number eight spot on SoundScan's top retail album chart. At the same time, the group's first international CD, *Backstreet Boys,* was still holding steady on the chart at number thirty-four—even though it had been released ten months before!

To no one's surprise, both albums continued to do phenomenally well in Canada. *Billboard* magazine reported that by December 1997 the first CD had sold more than 832,000 units since its October '96 release and the second one had already sold more than 529,000 copies. The Boys, as they had proved in Europe and Asia, were a smashing success on this side of the Atlantic as well. "Canada is definitely our leading market," Kevin told *Billboard* magazine's Larry LeBlanc. "We can't believe how incredible it's been here. Canadians were way ahead of the [U.S.] curve [in accepting the band]. The [Canadian breakthrough] initially came in Quebec from France."

Riding high on the success of their CD sales, the Boys hit the Canadian roads again with a tour from the end of December 1997 until early January 1998, hitting places such as Halifax, Quebec, Montreal, and Ottawa—again playing to sellout crowds, many of whom were seeing the Boys for the second or third time.

On December 31, 1997, the Backstreet Boys made front page news—for a good reason. The *Gazette*, a newspaper in Montreal, featured a story about the Boys and their five-day concert engagement in that city. As of that day, three out of five of the concerts had been sold out, including the first show at the Molson Centre on December 30. The arena holds fifteen thousand people, so by the time the five shows were over, close to seventy-five thousand people in and around Montreal saw BSB perform!

The Boys had given concerts in Montreal ten times in the previous year and a half, which provided lots of opportunities for old and new fans alike to catch their act. But according to repeat audience members, the shows just kept getting better and better—and the boys kept getting cuter and cuter! People who were interviewed by the reporter for the *Gazette* said that the Boys' slick dance moves were one of the top reasons they kept returning to additional concerts. Montrealers seemed to choose Nick as their favorite and Brian a close second.

People of all ages attended the concerts, again proving the wide appeal of the Boys and their cross-genre music. One forty-year-old woman stood outside of the Boys' hotel until three-thirty in the morning to try to get a glimpse of the group. Parents who were there with their kids recalled going to see the Beatles in concert when they were young and dragging along *their* parents, so they were more than happy to chaperone. But they came prepared with earplugs—not to drown out the music, most of the parents claimed, but to drown out the excited screams of the fans around them.

Much Music in Canada kicked off 1998 with BSB performing live on their *Intimate & Interactive* show on January 4, right in the middle of BSB's Canadian tour. More than a thousand fans started lining up on Queen Street West, outside of the MM studio, at 3 A.M.—and the show wasn't going on until 7 P.M. that night! Since many had waited sixteen hours in freezing rain and Canadian cold to see their Boys, the fans were naturally very excited when BSB finally took to the stage for their hour-and-a-half live performance and interview. The *Toronto Star* newspaper reported that the screaming was so loud that police and the staff of Much Music who were working outside had to wear earplugs! The *I&I* show was such a huge success that it was reaired two weeks later.

Preparing for the Final Attack

It had been a long but satisfying journey for the Boys. They had spent much of the last two years on the road, covering the United Kingdom, Europe, Asia, and Australia, and charming their fans wherever they went. Their first CD was multiplatinum in several countries, and the Backstreet Boys were enjoying the fruits of their labors. Since their CDs and singles had reached sales topping seven million, the Backstreet Boys were now in the big league. They had become one of the most popular, beloved, and successful musical groups of all time.

But they still had one major territory to conquer, one with which they were very familiar. In fact, it was a place all five Boys called home. It was the United States, looming large for them—the golden apple, the brass ring, the big kahuna. So, in the middle of 1997, riding high on their megasuccess all over the world, they turned their sights on America, determined to make it big at home. Far from it being a time to relax, the Boys went into overdrive, planning a triumphant and exciting return to the U.S. of A.

CHAPTER 3

Timing Is Everything

There is no question that the success of the Backstreet Boys is due to their extraordinary singing and dancing talents; their genre-crossing music; their catchy and memorable tunes, funky beats, and smooth sounds; their sweet harmonies; and—not least of all—their really, really hard work.

But of course the Backstreet Boys was not the first boy band to make the scene in the United States. There is a long history of all-male music singing groups popular with people between the ages of nine and nineteen. But as tastes, values, and society change, so does the music, which is one of the best mirrors to reflect the mood of the times. For example, in the 1960s, a lot of the music was about the horrors of the Vietnam War and pleas for world peace. In the 1970s music splintered into different types: hardcore rock and punk music was on one side, disco and soul music on another, and squeaky-clean family bands such as the Osmonds and the Jackson Five (as in Michael Jackson) were somewhere in the middle.

By the 1980s music had gone through another mood swing. The economy was good, the Baby Boom generation produced millions of yuppies (young urban professionals), and—probably most important—MTV debuted in 1981. All of this helped pave the way for pop music's comeback. MTV single-handedly revolutionized the music industry, making the form of the music video almost as important as the music itself. Soon only those artists who had an appealing or trendy image in addition to musical talent and a solid sound became stars. The "package" became crucial to being successful in the music business, and MTV-friendly boy bands were among those groups that succeeded in all three of those categories. New Edition, Menudo, and New Kids on the Block were just some of the all-male groups that reigned supreme during the late 1980s.

But then these groups started to fade in popularity in the early 1990s when the media and cultural critics identified Generation X—people born between 1964 and the early 1970s, who had grown up in a money-hungry, yuppie, brand-name-conscious society that made them pessimistic, negative, and disillusioned. This generation didn't go for upbeat messages—they wanted music to reflect their feelings of deep dissatisfaction with their parents, society, and the world, their slacker lifestyles, and their teenage angst about their lives. They found their voice in alternative and grunge music, which was made famous mostly by such bands as Nirvana and Pearl Jam. These bands and many others gave the members of Generation X songs filled with dark, negative messages and bitterness at having inherited a broken, mixed-up world. And until very recently, bands like Smashing Pumpkins, singers like

Alanis Morissette, and gangsta rap stars like Tupac Shakur were carrying on these gloomy, angry, or less-than-upbeat vibes.

This was the atmosphere and these were the artists of choice for American preteens and teenagers in 1995, when the Backstreet Boys released their first single, "We've Got It Goin' On." If the Backstreet Boys were as great then as they are now, why didn't this song take off like wildfire here in the States in 1995, as it did in England, Germany, and other points east and north?

One reason might be because in the United States, Top 40 radio stations and the national music video channels were still tuned into grunge and rap music, rewarding the heroes of those genres with loads of attention. The leaders in those two types of music had seen such immense success that many artists who came after them copied their styles and, as a result, got the bulk of the airplay. So when the Backstreet Boys tried to break into the music scene of the mid-1990s, the voices of younger music fans who were eager and ready for something different—namely, music that was softer and more upbeat—got drowned out by the wails and snarls of the stars who were making good money and a name for themselves out of their tortured spirits.

However, back in 1995, BSB's first U.S. single still made it onto *Billboard* magazine's Hot 100 chart—reaching number sixty-nine. Even though the song made it onto the chart, its position was a disappointment to the Backstreet Boys. Howie D. recently explained to a Reuters reporter his take on why the single didn't do better: "I think at the time . . . the scene wasn't exactly right for a style of group like us. Grunge was still heavily going, rap was really hard, and the pop scene wasn't really in phase at the time." The Boys knew they had a hit on their hands, but they also knew that breaking into the American music scene as it was at the time would be a huge uphill climb—perhaps impossible.

Take That!

Across the ocean, the music scene in the early 1990s was very different, mainly because grunge was a mostly American phenomenon and hadn't taken hold as strongly in the United Kingdom and Europe as it did in the United States. On the whole, pop music doesn't go in and out of style as much there as it does in the States—for some reason, the genre enjoys a steadier following across the Atlantic. The boy band Take That was formed in England in 1990 and then released their first CD, *Take That and Party,* in 1992. The CD went on to became a smashing success in the United Kingdom, winning all kinds of awards later that year and into 1993. Soon they were performing sold-out concerts all over Europe and the U.K.

But in 1995, even though the group was still doing phenomenally well with seven number one hits and was continuing to rack up more music awards, Robbie Williams, one of the most popular members, unexpectedly left the band, upsetting and confusing fans worldwide. The remaining four members tried to take up the mantle and keep going. Soon after, there was huge controversy between Williams and his former bandmates over whether he quit or was fired from the group. In February 1996, amidst rumors that the remaining Take That members were breaking up, the band held a press conference. They confirmed that in fact they were splitting up in April after they promoted their *Greatest Hits* album. This news shook the pop music world and devastated millions of devoted Take That fans, who publicly wept and mourned the loss of their top band at candlelit vigils worldwide. The last four members of the group performed their last single, "How Deep Is Your Love," at the British Music Awards a few days later. The song became Take That's eighth and last number one hit. (It's important to note that while Take That got some attention in the States in 1995 and 1996, ultimately they could not break through the blockade that grunge music had set up—even with their successful track record in Europe and elsewhere.)

As sad as the breakup of Take That was for many fans all over the world, it had done two important things for the Backstreet Boys: First, Take That had proven with their amazing success that there was a huge audience abroad for positive, harmony-heavy music; second, by breaking up, they left a huge, gaping space for a new boy group with a fresh new sound—an American sound, mixed with R&B, pop, gospel, and blues—the sound so skillfully and naturally adopted by the all-American Backstreet Boys.

When the Boys, their managers, and Jive Records

saw that grunge was still holding on in the United States and that in the United Kingdom and Europe pop music was still reigning supreme, thanks to Take That and also to the group Boyzone, they decided to concentrate their efforts to promote the Backstreet Boys abroad, where fans were ready for the next big thing. And happily, soon after setting sail across the Atlantic in 1995, the Backstreet Boys *became* the next big thing!

Sugar and Spice (and Three Blond Brothers) Make the Music Scene Nice

Meanwhile, back on the farm—or rather, back in the States—grunge was finally losing its grip on the music scene. Fans in flannel grew older and moved on to other things (college, jobs, and music with less screaming, such as Counting Crows and Hootie and the Blowfish). The fading interest in grunge not only affected the copycat bands who had tried to adopt the sound and style of their predecessors, but also it hurt the proven grunge heroes such as Pearl Jam. Nirvana had lost their lead singer, Kurt Cobain, who shot himself at the height of the band's career. The band never replaced him and faded from the scene, which also contributed to the eventual fall of grunge.

As 1996 turned into 1997, music on the radio waves and video channels started to lighten up at last. New, younger stars with positive, cleaner images started to break through, not only into the music scene, but also into television and movies. The music industry produced the first stars of what the media and cultural critics are calling "bubblegum pop." Who are these new, bright stars? Well, the Backstreet Boys, of course, who, after conquering practically the rest of the world, returned to the United States to release the single "Quit Playing Games (With My Heart)" in June 1997 and then their self-titled CD in August 1997 to an audience that was primed and ready for their smooth grooves, thanks to groups like the home-grown Hanson and the English imports the Spice Girls, who were enjoying their own newfound success on these shores. (Check out Chapter 4 for the whole story.)

Not coincidentally, according to the U.S. Census Bureau, there were thirty-seven million kids between the ages of ten and nineteen in the United States as of 1997, and the numbers are growing, expected to reach forty-two million during the next ten years—which is more teens than there have been in the last twenty-five years.

What do these numbers mean? They mean that the teenage population is becoming a big force in popular culture right now and that more and more music, tele-vision, movies, and stuff like clothes, magazines, and books will be geared to the prevailing tastes of this age group.

It is impossible to make a generalization about what it is that all the people in this generation want or to say that they want the same thing. However, it would be safe to say that the attitude of preteens and teenagers is more positive than it has been for a long while. It is also possible to say that this powerful new age group wants to see, listen to, and support artists who are their peers, who share their more positive outlooks, and who offer a melding of many different sounds, rather than fit into only one category of music. So when acts such as the teen jazz musician Jonny Lang, bubblegum pop stars Hanson, chanteuse Fiona Apple, country singer LeAnn Rimes, the Spice Girls, and Boyzone burst onto the scene in early 1997, the young market embraced them as their own.

Bob Moses, a music critic and coauthor of *You Stand There: Making Music Videos*, says that it is not a mystery that the Backstreet Boys and other popular groups such as the Spice Girls and Hanson have enjoyed such immense international success in the past couple of years. The kind of R&B-influenced dance-pop that the Backstreet Boys is so famous for is the kind of music that appeals to the widest, most diverse audiences and easily crosses cultural boundaries, he says. Since grunge has all but disappeared from the music scene, the mood in music in general has turned more optimistic. Rap music, for instance, which for a long time has been one of the edgiest types of music, has lightened up, becoming mellower, more melodic, and more heavily influenced by R&B. Record companies have seized upon changes in taste and overall outlook to promote artists that fit this new, more easygoing mood, such as Maxwell and Babyface.

"In addition," says Moses, "the international market has always been a singles-driven market, so dance-pop singles are what translates best to international audiences and therefore creates internationally-appealing stars, such as the Backstreet Boys." It is this "internationalization of tastes," as he calls it, that is the most interesting recent development in the music business. "The phenomenon of the music business creating teen idols goes back several years to the time of Bing Crosby and Frank Sinatra" (Bing was a heartthrob crooner in the 1930s and 1940s and Frank struck it big doing the same starting in the 1940s—he's still kicking today). "But ever since MTV came onto the scene in 1981 and Michael Jackson launched his solo career and made himself into a star by redefining the music video and playing to sold-out audiences all over the world, it has become much easier for artists to successfully cross many cultural boundaries with their music and accompanying videos and become true international music stars," concludes Moses.

And today, in addition to MTV and the scores of music video channels around the world, the World Wide Web and the Internet have further eroded international boundaries, allowing fans from Miami to Madrid, from San Francisco to Singapore, to share their common love for certain music groups by visiting each other's Web sites to get fan, tour, and concert information and by conversing with fellow fans all over the world in Internet chat rooms. With the speed, ease, and relatively low cost of using E-mail and electronic bulletin boards, word about who is hot travels fast—and far. There are hundreds of these virtual communities with members from dozens of countries built around their one common interest: their love of the Backstreet Boys' music.

So while the Boys were out of the country, singing

their hearts out to fans who spoke the international language of Backstreet in addition to their native languages of French, Spanish, Japanese, Hebrew, or whatever, these major shifts in both musical trends and population were taking place at home. Having kept their fingers on the pulse of American culture and letting their foreign fans send the word back to the States that these Boys just had to be heard, in 1997 the Backstreet Boys could at last prepare themselves to go home.

CHAPTER 4

Coming Home—
in a Big Way

It was time to come home. The Backstreet Boys had sold 5.4 million copies of their self-titled debut CD outside of the United States. The Boys had been playing to huge crowds all over the world. The level of their success was already beyond their wildest dreams. They had traveled the world and in a short time had seen dozens of countries that most people don't get to see in the course of a lifetime.

Everywhere they went, they had girls swooning for them. Everywhere they went, they had people clamoring for them to belt out one of their foot-stomping dance hits or sweetly harmonize on one of their most heart-wrenching ballads. Everywhere they went, they had mobs of fans dogging their every step, begging for an autograph or a kiss on the cheek. Everywhere, that is, except their own country.

Throughout the more than two years the Boys spent conquering the rest of the world, something still nagged at them. They wanted to be welcomed, accepted, and loved in their hometowns, in their home country, by their friends and fellow Americans. To them, this would be the height of success. And they wanted it—bad. So in 1997 the Boys headed back to familiar shores and went to work.

Backstreet Prepares to Go Back Home

During the time they were doing their thing abroad and touring doggedly throughout Europe, Asia, and Canada, they liked being able to make their periodic visits home to Orlando almost anonymously. They could just hang with their friends and family like regular kids, without attracting attention. But by the fall of 1997 they were totally up for being recognized here in the States. "We're ready to show everyone out there what we've got," Nick told *Tiger Beat*. However, the Boys did have some apprehensions about heading home. They knew what kind of hard work it took to make it big in other countries, so they were fully aware that becoming a success in the States was not automatic.

Since the group's popularity had first taken off abroad and then just kept skyrocketing, the Boys delayed their return to the United States and the release of their debut CD several times so they could meet the demands of their audiences in other countries. While the Boys were anxious to release their CD in the States, the delays actually gave them the chance to hone their craft and put together a somewhat different CD from the other two released outside America.

So in the early part of 1997, the Backstreet Boys hit the studio to record several new tracks. These new songs showcased their growth and experience during their career, the Boys' personal tastes, a little more of their own songwriting, and a mix of different sounds, such as smooth R&B, slamming dance tracks, midtempo songs, and ballads. Some of their new cuts were collaborations with well-known producers and songwriters, such as P.M. Dawn and Robert "Mutt" Lange, who wrote the Oscar-nominated song "I Finally Found Someone," which Barbra Streisand sang on the soundtrack for her movie *The Mirror Has Two Faces*.

In fact, the CD that the Backstreet Boys finally released in the United States in August of 1997, *Backstreet Boys,* was a different CD from either of the two that were released internationally. The U.S. release is a mix of some of BSB's first hit songs, recorded more than two years ago, and the newer tracks that they recorded in early 1997. So, in a way, the American fans have the best of the two CDs that were released abroad!

A couple of months before the full-length CD hit the U.S. stores, the Boys released their first single, "Quit Playing Games (With My Heart)," on June 10, 1997. Only a few weeks later, on June 28, the single jumped into the number twenty-four spot on *Billboard* magazine's Hot Shot Debut chart. It quickly bolted up the magazine's Hot 100 chart to the number six position and had sold fifty-eight thousand copies (according to SoundScan) by the middle of July 1997.

The radio stations all around the country were also digging BSB's groove in a big way. As early as May 1997, Top 40 and rhythm-crossover radio stations

were giving airtime to the Boys' fresh new single.
New York's Z-100 and WPRO in Providence, Rhode
Island, were among the first U.S. radio stations to
jump on the BSB bandwagon.

U.S. Fans Jump on the BSB Bandwagon

Word about BSB spread fast. Once fans got their
first taste of the Boys' sweet voices and memorable
lyrics, they wanted more and more. If they couldn't
find their favorite BSB vid on MTV, fans started
requesting them on The Box, a caller-request music
video cable channel. This caused the video for "Quit
Playing Games" to debut as that channel's most
requested video.

"Quit Playing Games" easily became one of the
most memorable and favorite songs of the summer
of 1997. The single moved up to the top three on
Billboard magazine's singles chart and stayed there
for three months. (Nick admits it is one of his favorite
BSB songs and he still hasn't gotten sick of it!) It
also jumped onto other U.S. music charts, such as
Rick Dees's Top 40 and Casey Kasem's Top 40.
Eventually the single went platinum in the United
States, proving the Boys were definitely *not* playing
games when it came to making their return to the
States a triumphant one.

To get their new American fans pumped for the
release of BSB's CD and increase audience awareness
about the group, they distributed a limited amount of
special official BSB merchandise. Fans who were on

their toes could have snapped up one of sixty-five thousand BSB sampler cassettes that were distributed with a Love Stories series of teen romance books from Bantam Books or mailed to those kids who subscribe to the Sweet Valley High book series. In August 1997 JC Penney also made BSB cassette music samplers available with the purchase of Kaboodles makeup cases. Some of you who visited the national department store late in the summer of 1997 might have also seen BSB videos played on special screens in the junior department. There was plenty of other good BSB stuff that was given away exclusively to the rapidly growing number of U.S. fans: other cassette samplers came with BSB temporary tattoos, and a limited-edition CD single came with postcard pinups.

Features about the Boys started appearing in all the biggest teen magazines, such as *16*, *Tiger Beat*, and *Teen Machine* so fans could read about their favorite new group. The magazines held contests giving fans the opportunity to meet the Boys at their concerts or store appearances. To help the editors of *Teen Beat* magazine get to know the latest heartthrobs of the music scene, Bill Bellamy, a VJ from MTV, brought BSB to the *Teen Beat* offices. Along with several articles introducing the Boys to new American fans, these mags also included plenty of pictures of the hunky fivesome, as well as pull-out posters so people could have their favorite BSBer on their bedroom walls and lockers. BSB American mania had begun!

So by the time their self-titled *Backstreet Boys* CD was released on August 12, 1997, American fans were ready for it. The review of the CD in *People* magazine said, "[The] Backstreet Boys sing like they're having a ball. Already international megastars, with more than 11 million albums sold outside the U.S., the Orlando-based quintet has struck gold at home with the Top 5 single 'Quit Playing Games (With My Heart).' "

On the day of the CD release, Z-100, a Top 40 radio station, hosted a major press conference for the Backstreet Boys in New York City at the All-Star Café in the famous, bustling Times Square. The Boys unfortunately were a little late because they had been busy doing a sound check next door at the Virgin Megastore, where the Boys were scheduled to perform a few songs later.

Back at the All-Star, three hundred reporters and photographers—not only from all over the United States but also from other parts of the world (including Australia) where BSB was already hugely popular—had gathered. While the reporters were waiting for the Boys to come in, some foreign press people got up to talk about how big the Backstreet Boys were in their own countries. Meanwhile, a huge group of eager fans was gathering outside the Virgin store to wait for the Boys to perform.

When the Boys finally did arrive at the press conference, they fielded all kinds of interesting questions, about everything from Brian's $50 waterbed (it's true, he bought a used waterbed for $50 and sleeps in it whenever he is home) to what it's like touring all over the world. One reporter asked them how it felt to finally be getting tons of attention at home. Nick responded, "It feels sooooooooooooo wonderful! It is truly what we have been dreaming about." When asked if the Boys have a special message for their U.S. fans, Howie answered, "We will be doing our best all the time! We hope to be an act that has something for everyone." Then they showed the reporters their videos, including the one for their song "Everybody (Backstreet's Back)." The president of Jive Records presented the Boys with plaques that commemorated their album shipping gold and the single being certified gold in the United States. After the conference, the Boys headed next door to the Virgin Megastore to perform "Everybody," an a cappella version of "Just To Be Close," "As Long As You Love Me," and their gold number one hit, "Quit Playing Games (With My Heart)."

Bringing It Home at Last

A couple of days later, the Boys headed south to do an event at Universal Studios in Florida, then took a couple of days off before taking off to Austria and Germany for a couple of weeks of appearances and shows. Even while doing their fancy footwork in the States, the Boys didn't let their loyal foreign fans down.

To say thank you to their American fans for welcoming them home and to announce their biggest, much-anticipated, long-time-in-the-works U.S. tour, the Boys gave a free concert in New York City. "I'd say this is a big dream come true," A.J. told *Tiger Beat* magazine. "We'd never really gotten a chance to be here for the last year and a half. Now we're finally bringing it home." This was their biggest U.S. tour yet and they were very excited to be able to play for their family and friends at long last.

As a way to celebrate the return of the Backstreet Boys, their hometown newspaper, the *Orlando Sentinel*, held a Meet the Backstreet Boys Contest in August 1997. Fans were asked to call the newspaper's hotline to tell why they should win the chance to meet the Boys in person. The hotline received calls from several hundred fans of all ages, but only two lucky winners were chosen: Staci Rankin, a nine-year-old student from Orlando, and Taryn Rivera, a twelve-year-old from Kissimmee.

How did these two clever girls win the contest? Staci left a sweet message saying, "One day I'm going to marry you one of you and I thought you would want to meet your future wife." That must have gotten the judges' attention! Taryn, on the other hand, spent an hour and a half working with her best friend on a poem that they wrote especially for the Boys. It went like this: "A.J., Brian, Nick, Howie, and Kevin / Meeting them would be like heaven / Because if we met them you would see / The happiest two girls in Kis-sim-mee."

The two winners with their guests (so Taryn's best friend didn't get left behind!) got to meet the Boys during their appearance at the Fundango Street Festival at Universal Studios Florida on Friday, August 15, 1997. BSB also scheduled an appearance at a local Blockbuster on the following day.

The two events were huge successes, with major

fan turnouts for both. A reporter from the *Orlando Sentinel* admitted that Boys were much better-looking in person, with smiles that were "knee-buckling." She went on to say, "These guys are so nice it's a wonder our contest winners weren't carried away in stretchers after meeting them at Universal Studios' Fundango Fest on Friday." Looks like the Boys made a new fan!

On September 19, 1997, the Boys headed to the West Coast to appear at the Last Chance Summer Dance, hosted by Kiss-FM radio in Long Beach, California. They performed with Robyn, Nu Flavor, Wild Orchid, and Third Party.

But the Boys' first major home-turf concert was on September 21, 1997, at the Tupperware Auditorium in Kissimmee, Florida—not far from the Magic Kingdom. It only made sense that they were kicking off their biggest U.S. tour in their hometown, since that is where they started in 1993. Just as their manager, Louis J. Pearlman, had predicted four years earlier, the Boys came back to Orlando as huge stars.

This is a large venue that has hosted concerts for several nationally known acts. But not only was this a special concert for the arena, because it was hosting the area's own local heroes, it was also special for the Boys, because it was the biggest American venue they had played thus far. The Backstreet Boys had certainly come a long way since 1993, when they started out performing in high-school gyms.

Not surprisingly, BSB's September 21 near-sellout homecoming show was a huge success. It took a half hour for the Boys to finally take the stage, during which many of the fans were screaming for the Boys to come out. But it was worth the wait. The Boys first appeared posed very sexily all around the stage, causing the fans to stand on their seats to get a better view and scream even louder. BSB stayed onstage for an hour, singing their hit ballads, like "I'll Never Break Your Heart" and "All I Have To Give," and their dance tracks, like "We've Got It Goin' On" and "Get Down (You're The One For Me)." The Boys also danced like crazy, showing off their hottest moves. Nick seemed to be the favorite—or at least, his fans were the most vocal. The concert review by Parry Gettelman in the *Orlando Sentinel* declared, "The Boys are all real pros, and they harmonized exceptionally well, especially in two a cappella segments." With this first concert hailed as a success, the Boys could confidently move forward and continue taking the United States by storm.

It Might Have Been the Fall, but Things Were Just Heating Up

By the time the Boys headed back north to New York City, BSB mania had reached a fevered pitch. The *New York Daily News* reported a Beatlemania-type flashback: On Tuesday, September 30, after the Backstreet Boys made an appearance at the Motown Café, approximately three hundred fans chased them down Fifty-seventh Street in busy midtown Manhattan!

That same night, the Backstreet Boys hit the stage

in New York City to perform for a huge crowd at the Hammerstein Ballroom. Brian admitted that even though the group had done hundreds of shows before this one, he was still very nervous right before the curtain went up because not only was this one of their first U.S. shows, it was also New York City! He felt himself freezing up, but once the music started, he felt much more comfortable. The Boys entertained their screaming fans with live renditions of "I'd Do Anything For You" and of course their biggest U.S. hit, "Quit Playing Games (With My Heart)." They also treated their fans to their famous sweet a cappella singing and some slamming dance moves. They changed costumes three times, wearing at one point white sexy silky PJs, baring their buff chests to their adoring fans.

Soon fans could show their Backstreet pride online. In November 1997 the Backstreet Boys launched a brand-new official Backstreet Boys Web site, www.backstreetboys.com. Fans went wild for this new site. In the first day alone, the site received over 100,000 hits, which caused the system to shut down three times over its first weekend. As news of the cool new site spread, the number of one-day hits swelled to 130,000, causing the system to choke a few more times. The Web site features all kinds of great info about the Boys, including the latest news, cool pictures, music clips, bios about each BSBer, BSB merchandise, a chat room, and a premium pay service for VIPs, which was launched in late November 1997.

The fall of 1997 proved that not only could the Boys perform onstage and have the stamina to travel all over the world for long stretches of time, but they could also successfully master a balancing act that only the most energetic and heartiest could handle. While their TV appearances were being aired in the States, the Boys were still touring like mad abroad. They went to Paris, Madrid, Sopressa, and London— just in the last couple weeks of November! It was important to the Boys that their fans abroad didn't think that they were going to forget about them just because the group was launching its return to the United States.

Meanwhile, back in the good ol' U.S. of A., the Boys released their second single, the slower and more romantic "As Long As You Love Me," which joined its mate on the U.S. music charts. The new single was played on CHR as well as rhythm-crossover radio stations all over the country, proving the song's wide audience appeal. The video for this song also made a good showing on The Box, holding the number five spot in early November. In addition, the video was aired on M2, MTV's all-music-video channel, as well as on the original MTV. And three months after the initial release of their self-titled CD in America, sales had reached the half-million mark.

Soon the Boys were everywhere. In October, November, and December they were all over TV. *American Journal*, the national newsmagazine show, did a profile about the Boys and their newfound success at home on October 3, 1997, proclaiming that the Backstreet Boys were here to stay. The Boys showed up on the *Today* show and *Vibe*. On November 14, 1997, they appeared on the *Ricki Lake Show* and hosted

ABC's Friday-night lineup from a sunny beach, during which the fivesome joked around, sang some bits of their songs, and introduced the popular prime-time TV shows *Sabrina, the Teenage Witch* and *Boy Meets World*. On November 22 they took a ride on *Soul Train*, the dance show that features performances by major artists. The Boys even got to ride on a float and perform a song in the famous Macy's Thanksgiving Day Parade in New York City.

They continued to make major appearances through December. On December 8 they were presenters on the *Billboard* Awards show. The Backstreet Boys were also part of the all-star lineup for the Jingle Ball concert at Madison Square Garden hosted by Z-100 (WHTZ), New York City's Top 40 radio station. The Wallflowers, another group to hit it big in 1997, and rock veterans Aerosmith were also part of this annual Christmas concert celebration.

On Christmas Day 1997, the Boys got one of the biggest presents of all: BSB was the special guest on the fifteenth annual *A Magical Walt Disney World Christmas*! This was a true homecoming celebration, not only because they were in Florida, where they'd gotten together, but also because they were coming back to Disney World as superstars! The Christmas extravaganza was hosted by TGIF stars Melissa Joan Hart, star of *Sabrina, the Teenage Witch*, and Ben Savage, star of *Boy Meets World*. For this TV special, the Boys performed their holiday favorite, "Christmastime." They also sang "As Long As You Love Me" from the Castle Stage, in the heart of the Magic Kingdom. And on ABC TV's Web site during the entire holiday season, www.abc.com, fans could download a special holiday greeting from the Backstreet Boys.

By the end of the year, the Backstreet Boys had firmly established themselves as one of the hottest music groups in America. "Quit Playing Games (With My Heart)" garnered the number eleven position on *Billboard* magazine's year-end chart, Hot 100 Singles for 1997, one notch below "Wannabe" by the Spice Girls and one notch above Hanson's "MMMBop"!

Somebody Stop Me!

It was the end of 1997, but the Boys showed no signs that they were going to slow down. The last few days of the old year and the first few of the new were filled with major dates in Canada, including Montreal, Quebec, Halifax, and Toronto. (Head to Chapter 12 for an exclusive review of the January 3, 1998, BSB concert at the Skydome in Toronto by Jessica Horwood, creator of the Web site Picke Bicke's BSB Haven!) After celebrating A.J.'s birthday on January 9, the Boys kicked off their second U.S. tour, beginning in Greensboro, North Carolina, on January 14, with dates in Charlotte, North Carolina; Atlanta, Georgia; Louisville, Kentucky; Detroit, Michigan; Tampa and West Palm Beach in Florida; Providence, Rhode Island; and Albany, New York—all before Nick's birthday on January 28!

In between, they presented at the American Music Awards on January 26 before continuing with some more U.S. dates after that in Plainview, New York; Indianapolis, Indiana; Kansas City, Kansas; and Dallas, Texas.

The group also got lots of ink in early 1998. They were profiled in the February 1998 issues of both *YM* and *Teen* magazines. *YM* even offered the chance for one reader to win a ticket to a Backstreet Boys concert—and get serenaded by the Boys onstage!

Spring 1998 sent the Boys back overseas again to France, Ireland, England—including playing two shows at London's famous Wembley Stadium—Sweden, Finland, Belgium, Norway, Holland, and back to Spain. During this tour, they made a stop in Germany to return to VIVA's studios to tape an *Unplugged* on March 28. After finishing out the European tour, the Boys headed home in time for American high-school graduations to do a number of late-spring engagements for the Magic Kingdom Grad Nights in the state where they got their start.

Was there any downside to all this fame and recognition at home? Privacy, or rather the lack thereof, is the one thing the Boys agree is the only less-than-great part of their success. Even when the Boys were drawing crowds of thousands to their concerts and appearances in other parts of the world, for a long time they could walk around just about anywhere in the States and not get recognized. While the Boys love the attention they get from fans, it was nice to be able to come home every once in a while and be not a Backstreet Boy but simply A.J. or Howie—regular guys.

But now all that has changed—probably forever. With the megasuccess of their CD *Backstreet Boys* came a growing number of devotees who followed them around, called their homes, or mobbed them when they arrived at airports, screaming their names from behind barricades, begging for one autograph.

But if that's the price of fame, the Boys agree, they are more than happy to pay.

PART TWO

Let's Hear It
for the Boys!

CHAPTER 5

Kevin Richardson: The Group's Unofficial Leader

Vital Stats

Full name: Kevin Scott Richardson
Hair: Black
Eyes: Blue-green
Height: 6'
Weight: 155 lbs.
Shoe size: 11¹/₂
Nicknames: Kev, Train, Mr. Body Beautiful, Kevy-Kev
Birthplace: Lexington, Kentucky
Residence: Orlando, Florida
Birth date: October 3, 1971
Astrological sign: Libra
Marital status: Single
Family Status: Parents Ann and Jerald (his father died in 1991); older brothers Jerald junior and Tim
Pets: Quincy, a cat

Roots

Kevin, the oldest member of the Backstreet Boys, is a farm boy who grew up almost like a modern-day pioneer. Until Kevin was nine years old, he and his family—parents Ann and Jerald and older brothers Jerald junior and Tim—lived on a ten-acre farm in Kentucky. After that, the Richardson family moved into a modern log cabin, also in Kentucky, where they lived for the next eight years. Talk about being an all-American boy!

Kevin remembers his childhood with fondness, since he was very close to his family and spent his years as a young boy doing all sorts of fun things, like riding horses and dirt bikes and playing Little League baseball. He loved school, too.

From a very early age he was a good singer and would spend lots of time in front of his bedroom mirror singing into a hairbrush-cum-microphone. To encourage this natural talent, his parents gave him a set of keyboards when he was in his first year of high school, which Kevin then played at restaurants and weddings. His desire to be an entertainer only grew, and soon he was spending more of his free time singing. During high school he also joined the drama club and chorus, and entered local talent shows as well. He had parts in local theater for shows such as *Bye Bye Birdie* and *Barefoot in the Park.* Kevin feels indebted to his family, because even from the very beginning, they were encouraging and supportive of his career.

After graduating from high school, Kevin was torn

between joining the air force and pursuing his music career. But his father told him that he should follow what was in his heart, so Kevin dedicated himself full time to music and entertaining. For a time he was in a local Top 40 cover band, but not only was this experience less than satisfying, it wasn't getting him anywhere. Kevin knew that if he was really serious about his career, he would have to move to a place where there were more serious opportunities in entertainment.

So in late 1990 he packed up his bags, said good-bye to his family, and headed south to Orlando and Disney World, where a lot of movies and TV shows were beginning to be produced and filmed. The first job Kevin landed was as a tour guide for Disney World. This job not only got him closer to what he was looking for, it also allowed him some time to do his songwriting and practice his music. Eventually he landed other jobs at Disney, such as playing a Teenage Mutant Ninja Turtle and Aladdin onstage and in daily parades.

When Kevin was about nineteen, his parents and two older brothers came down from Kentucky to visit him for vacation, which he says was a great time. What the family didn't know was that this vacation would be one of their last happy times together.

Right after that, Kevin's father, Jerald, who was only forty-nine years old, was diagnosed with colon cancer. At first his parents didn't tell Kevin the news. His dad had surgery to remove the tumor right away, and since the survival rate with early detection and treatment is usually pretty high, his dad didn't want to worry Kevin by telling him. Unfortunately, the surgery didn't do the trick, because the cancer had already spread through his father's entire body. Kevin was devastated by the news and moved back home to Kentucky to be with his dad. His oldest brother, Jerald junior—named after their father— also moved home from Dallas, where he worked as a model.

By living at home, Kevin was able to help out around the house and care for his father. He also saw firsthand the toll the disease was taking on his father's health. The chemotherapy treatment his father was getting produced clots in his blood, which caused him to suffer a stroke. Luckily, his father lived through this experience, though it was a setback in his recovery.

Before he had gotten sick, his father had been a very active, outdoorsy guy. Jerald Richardson was tall and strong. When he was young he had played football. He was very handy around the house, and he could fix anything. He was not a complainer, even if he hurt himself or was sick. He was strong and dependable, so it was hard for Kevin to see his father in his ill and weakened state.

Through the entire ordeal, his mom remained strong, although it was very tough on her, for she and Kevin's dad had even been high-school sweethearts!

Kevin's family was and is very close, so they were very supportive of each other during his father's illness. But, Kevin admitted, "I was very angry. I felt my father had been cheated of his golden years. My brothers and I were growing up, sorting out our own lives. He should finally have been able to sit back, get ready to retire, and do what he wanted. But he was taken away. He was only 49."

Sadly, Kevin's father only lived ten months after his initial diagnosis and died on August 26, 1991.

Seven years later, Kevin still misses his dad in many ways, especially during the holidays, which were always happy times for the Richardson family. His father had encouraged Kevin to pursue his interest in music, even though originally Kevin thought he should be practical and join the air force after high school. His father believed it was important that his son do whatever he wanted to do, which is probably where Kevin gets his philosophy about pursuing one's dreams.

As Kevin moves forward and lives his life, he thinks of his dad and tries to do things that would make Jerald senior proud. "As long as I do what makes me happy, without sacrificing my morals, and follow what I was brought up to believe, he'll be proud."

In honor of his late father, Kevin dedicated the U.S. CD to him. Kevin wrote the last part of his thanks in the liner notes about his father's death in a frank and heartfelt way that clearly shows Kevin's continuing love and respect for the father he still sorely misses. Calling him the "greatest man" he would ever know, he said, "If I can be half the man you were as a Father, a Husband & as a Friend, then I will consider myself to be successful."

Up Close and Personal

Considering Kevin's personal tragedy and the fact that he is the oldest group member, it is no wonder that he is probably the most mature and is considered the group's unofficial leader. Kevin believes himself to be sincere and serious about his work. Others say Kevin can also be a bit on the mysterious side, which is probably due in part to the pain he still feels from the loss of his father. Through thick and thin, though, Kevin is a confident and mature professional who is just as respectful to his fans as he is with his friends and family.

Kevin likes being the oldest in the group because he can be the big brother to all the guys (which is the opposite of his family situation, since he is the youngest of three brothers). The other four BSBers tend to look up to Kevin because he is the oldest and has the most serious side of all of them.

Cousin Brian has said that he thinks Kev is a perfectionist, which sometimes hides his other positive characteristics. He says that Kevin is aware that he needs to chill out sometimes, sit back, and let things be. If Kevin is unhappy with something, people know it— not because he rants and raves, but because he might give people a particular stern look that means he is not pleased. Kevin also won't put up with arrogant or conceited people—that attitude is something he doesn't understand and would rather not deal with.

Howie has said that of the fivesome, he considers Kevin to be the authoritative, mature, professional, and responsible one. Kevin knows what he wants but apparently sometimes gets frustrated because he is not sure of the best, most efficient way to achieve his goals. He is careful, however, not to come across as if he is bossing everyone around or telling them what to do.

Which two BSBers are most likely to engage in a friendly tiff? Apparently Kevin and Nick, which might be due in part to the fact that Kev is the oldest band member and Nick is the youngest.

People tell the dark and handsome Kevin that he looks like a younger Clint Black, the country music star, which Kev takes as a compliment, especially because he appreciates country music more than any of the other four guys. People probably also make this association because Kevin has an obvious southern accent, like his cousin Brian. Kevin actually gets his dark, rugged looks from being a mix of many nationalities, including Cherokee, Irish, Italian, and English.

Kevin feels that since the entertainment biz on the whole is so totally looks-conscious, it is important to keep himself looking his best—not only because it is expected by the media and his fans, but also because working out and eating right make him *feel* good. In fact, he loves when the band is really getting into it during a concert—when they are really hot and kicking up the sweat. Those are usually the times when he feels the happiest.

Secret Scoop

Kevin confesses that he wishes he had A.J.'s voice, which he thinks has a cool, raspy, soul-funk quality to it. He also admires his cousin Brian's voice because he thinks it has a smoothness to it, like Kenny Loggins's voice.

Kevin has a weakness for peanut butter. He likes peanut butter on just about anything (!), though his favorite combo is pretty traditional: PB&J on some Ritz crackers. "I could eat those babies all day!" says Kev.

Besides Kevin's serious side, he also can be a bit of a softy. This tall, strong guy wouldn't mind a hug every day. Kev also admits that he cries when he watches sad movies. His grandpa is also sentimental, which is where Kevin thinks he gets his soft side from. Since Kevin really misses his family when he is away on tour, he takes an envelope full of snapshots of them wherever he goes. And when the BSB's CD went gold, he bawled like a little baby!

Kevin also adores children. He pays extra-special attention to his youngest fans; he will always give them an autograph or pose for pictures with them.

Why is one of Kev's nicknames "Train"? One reason is because when he was a linebacker for his high-school football team in Lexington, he was really good at running over people like a train! A.J. said that they call Kevin "Train" because sometimes he goes on "automatic pilot" and just plows through people—especially when he is playing b-ball. Either way, it alludes to Kevin's being strong in mind, body, and spirit.

Other secret nicknames for Kev? Pumpkin and Boo—but no one will offer any explanations there.

Love Life Sitch

Kevin is an old-fashioned kind of guy when it comes to girls. He was brought up to be polite and respectful of women, so he totally believes in opening the car door for a woman, pulling her chair out for her to sit down, and letting her order first—acting just like a classic gentleman would. It is exactly these kind of mature actions that have people calling Kevin "Mr. Sophisticated." He even likes champagne! Because of his traditional values, he is not very attracted to girls who use harsh language or who don't have the best manners.

But while Kev minds his p's and q's and can show a girl the utmost respect, he can be shy at first. To counter his shyness, he prefers to be friends with a woman he is interested in, so they can get to know each other first and see if they like each other enough to start dating. Unfortunately, the group's current hectic schedule doesn't allow for much of this kind of extended, low-key courtship.

When Kevin was nineteen, he was engaged to a girl named Beth. But they eventually broke off the engagement because they both felt that they were too young for marriage.

The sweetest thing that a girl has ever done for Kevin happened once when he was really sick. The girl he was dating got a chicken soup recipe from her mom, made the soup from scratch, and brought it to him. Now that is *sweet*.

Kevin thinks that what would make him a great boyfriend is his honesty. He is not a game-player, meaning he will just say what he thinks—though thoughtfully and respectfully. He also says he thinks it is really sexy when a girlfriend borrows his clothes and wears them. He claims that he prefers a girl to be wearing something way oversized rather than some really revealing miniskirt or tight, low-cut top. He wants to be with someone who he can talk to. A nice smile doesn't hurt either, he adds.

Currently, Kevin says, he is single but dating. But given the packed BSB schedule, it doesn't look like he'll have much time to do even that!

Future Holdings

Kevin has been playing the piano for a very long time, but now he is getting into some songwriting as well. He has also started learning how to play bass guitar. He says he is interested not only in singing music, but also in playing, writing, producing, working in the studio—all of it. Eventually he will want to be able to do something different in music from what he is currently doing, so he is paving the way now by learning as much as he can. Also, learning more about music helps him with his songwriting, because it is important to know about rhythm in order to write music.

Someday Kevin hopes to star in a movie and get back to doing some more serious acting than what he was doing at Disney before the days of BSB.

More 411 on Kevin

Favorite color: Blue (as in Kentucky, the Bluegrass State)

Favorite foods: Mom's home cooking, especially her chili, pancakes, and waffles; Mexican and Asian food

Favorite sports: Football, lifting weights, horseback riding, water skiing, swimming, surfing, basketball, and hockey

Instruments: Keyboards, piano

Favorite music: Prince (the Artist Formerly Known As . . .), Elton John (whose songs he sometimes plays on his keyboards during concerts), R. Kelly, Babyface, Michael Jackson, Teddy Riley, Billy Joel, the Eagles, Brian McKnight, classical and soul music, a little country music (such as music by Clint Black)

Favorite movies: *Top Gun* and *The Shawshank Redemption*

Favorite actress: Nicole Kidman

Dream women: Liv Tyler, Michelle Pfeiffer, and Demi Moore

Favorite actors: John Travolta, Tom Cruise

Favorite TV shows: *Roseanne* and *Martin* (Kevin is "over" *The Simpsons*)

Favorite book: *Interview with the Vampire*, by Anne Rice

Accessories: An assortment of silver rings on both hands (he moves them around); silver bracelets and two black leather bracelets on his right wrist; earrings, both hoops and studs

Favorite colognes: Paco and XS by Paco Rabanne

Favorite hobbies: When he is not working, Kevin can be out club hopping, dancing, or doing all kinds of outdoor sports, from water skiing and surfing to camping and dirt biking

Worst habit: Sleeping late

What he looks for in a girl: Kevin is attracted to women who are accepting of him the way he is; he considers himself to be shy, which sometimes makes him worry about what he is going to say or what people will think about what he says

Experience: Before joining BSB, he worked at Disney World both as a guide and as Aladdin, a Teenage Mutant Ninja Turtle, and Prince Eric in the *Little Mermaid* show

Favorite saying: "What's up?"

Odd facts: Kevin lived in a log cabin for eight years, and he is also a certified ballroom dance instructor

He's most likely to: Encourage people to follow their dreams, because he believes that your dreams can come true

What he thought he was going to be before BSB: A pilot

What Kevin says: About touring—"A lot of fun, a lot of work, and sometimes a little lonely. It's what I've always dreamed of!"; about recording in the studio—"Sing. Eat. Sing. Sing. Eat. Sing. *Sleep!*"

CHAPTER 6

A.J. McLean: The Talker

Vital Stats

Full name: Alexander James McLean
Hair: Brown (though since A.J. likes to experiment with
     different hair colors, you never know when he is
     going to have platinum blond hair)
Eyes: Brown
Height: 5'9"
Weight: 147 lbs.
Shoe size: 10 $^1/_2$
Nicknames: A.J., Bone, Mr. Cool
Birthplace: West Palm Beach, Florida
Residence: Kissimmee, Florida
Birth date: January 9, 1978
Astrological sign: Capricorn
Marital status: Single
Family status: Parents Denise and Bob (divorced); A.J.'s an
     only child
Pets: Toby Wan Kenobi, a dachshund

Roots

A.J. was born in West Palm Beach, Florida, on January 9, 1978. A.J. was four years old and an only child when his parents got divorced. One night his father left without a word, and A.J. never saw him again. This dramatic event caused a lot of pain for A.J. and his mom, but ultimately made them very close as a result.

A.J. probably would have become a writer or a poet if he hadn't gone into showbiz first. (In fact, he has talents for both of those other things, and you never know—he still could do them!) Luckily for his fans, though, his mom recognized A.J.'s talent for singing and dancing when he was very young and encouraged him to do as much as he could.

A.J.'s first acting job was as Dopey in *Snow White* when he was just a kid. That part was only the beginning. Amazingly, A.J. had already appeared in twenty-seven plays and musicals by the time he was in sixth grade! He acted in classics such as the *Nutcracker*, *Fiddler on the Roof*, and *The King and I*. Then, when he was in junior high, he began his television career by landing parts in Nickelodeon's *Hi Honey, I'm Home* and *Welcome Freshman*.

During this time in his life, A.J. also took acting, dance, and singing lessons to build on his natural talents. When A.J. was fourteen, he met Howie D. through his vocal coach, since they both had the same one. After that, the two guys became friends and started to hang out and go to auditions together. The two then met Nick at other auditions.

To join BSB in 1993, both Nick and A.J. turned down offers to be in the Mickey Mouse Club. A.J. was still attending school when he joined BSB, so like Nick and Brian, A.J. needed to have a private tutor to help him continue and finish his studies.

Denise, A.J.'s mom, is his best gal. She has also adopted the Backstreet Boys in more ways than one: She is very involved with the group and helps arrange their schedules, goes with them on tours sometimes, and has even started some of their fan clubs in other countries.

Up Close and Personal

Besides being in BSB, one of A.J.'s favorite things to do is talk—a lot. He is a regular chatterbox, actually. A.J. knows that sometimes he yaks too much. A.J. also spends lots of time on the phone talking to friends and family, especially when the Boys are away on tour. While the Boys love him for his constant storytelling, they also get tired of it at times. Apparently, when the Boys first started touring, A.J. and Brian used to have to share a hotel room. But the thing was that A.J. wouldn't stop talking and sometimes drove Brian a bit crazy. Luckily, now each of them gets his own room when they are away touring, which is a relief to Brian.

A.J., who would describe himself as "freaky, funky, and romantic," is also a self-admitted ham— he likes to do all kinds of crazy stuff to have fun, whether he is on or off the stage. One time A.J. had to wear a costume of "The Riddler" (the character who appears in *Batman*) for a photo shoot—it was totally green spandex, à la Jim Carrey. So he borrowed the costume and went out onstage in it that night to introduce the two opening acts for their concert. The audience went totally wild, and the guys couldn't believe he had the guts to do that. They all thought it was pretty funny.

Even when he is offstage, A.J. doesn't stop hamming it up. This BSBer is definitely not a shy guy— he loves to be the center of attention, whether he is telling a long, colorful story to a group of people or reciting poetry to girls. Howie and the other guys tease A.J. all the time about his poetic, romantic, attention-loving side.

A.J. has a serious side, too. Actually, A.J. writes his own poetry, which often becomes the inspiration for his songwriting. Since A.J.'s favorite school subject was English, it makes sense that he loves to read and write. He is considered the intellectual one in the group, because during his down time he can often be found reading Shakespeare, T. S. Eliot, or Edgar Allan Poe—all of whose work influences A.J.'s own writing. This romantic also likes to paint when he gets the chance. When A.J. gets some quiet time for himself, he plays some soothing music, turns off the lights, lies back, and relaxes for an hour or so. If he has a lot of energy and needs to let off some steam, he says that shooting pool or playing a little b-ball helps him feel better.

When people have problems and they want to talk to somebody, A.J. is the man—he is a great listener.

The downside is that he sometimes has trouble keeping secrets! He also admits that of all the Boys, he is the biggest worrywart and can sometimes be a bit impatient.

Kevin thinks that A.J. is a softy. A.J. doesn't like to say "no" to anyone because he doesn't like to upset others. As a result, he makes too many promises he can't necessarily keep.

A.J. and Nick are very close, probably because they are the youngest band members. They also share the same birthday month, January, which every year gives them a great excuse to throw a joint birthday party. One year Nick and A.J. threw themselves a giant birthday bash at their manager's house. The party was to celebrate Nick's sixteenth birthday and A.J.'s eighteenth. They had about two hundred friends there, and it was kickin'! The Birthday Boys got a little nutty and decided to have some fun with each other: A.J. mushed birthday cake all over Nick—even in his hair and on his shirt—and then the guys threw A.J. in the pool with all his clothes on! The place ended up being a mess, since the blowout party didn't end until the wee hours of the morning.

A.J., always the party animal, loves to go out dancing in nightclubs. One time he went dancing in Paris at a club that is an artsy hangout; it plays '70s and hip-hop music. He stayed out until four-thirty in the morning, even though the Boys were scheduled to leave on a flight at five-thirty that same morning! Not surprisingly, they ended up missing that flight and had to run around like crazy that day to make up for it. You gotta pay to play, that's for sure.

A.J. has lots of girls who are "just friends." He says he has more female friends than guy friends because most of his guy friends are heavily into the sports thing, which isn't the only thing he is interested in doing or talking about. When he hangs with his female friends, they go shopping—buying phat stuff, clothes, and whatever.

Another nickname for A.J. might be "Mr. Flash," because he is probably the most extravagant of the Boys. He loves clothes, funky accessories, and big jewelry. A.J. is always seen sporting one of his several pairs of dark sunglasses and gold earrings. A.J. also collects hats, which he wears when he is trying to keep a low profile in public.

A.J. would like to get some tattoos. He once said that he would want a really big one on his back, between his shoulder blades, in the form of a sun. On his left arm he would get his nickname, "Bone," and then on his right arm he would get a word in Japanese that means "eternal life." He also wouldn't mind getting his eyebrow pierced. It seems A.J. doesn't have a fear of pain!

An interviewer from *Live and Kicking* magazine once asked A.J. which three stars he fantasizes about inviting to a party. A.J.'s answer: Jim Carrey, because he is so funny; Geri from the Spice Girls, because she knows how to be crazy; and Geena Davis, because A.J. has harbored a crush on her for the longest time. Those answers certainly reflect all the different sides of this BSBer's personality!

Secret Scoop

Why is A.J.'s nickname "Bone"? A security guard once called A.J. "Bone" because he is so skinny. The name stuck.

Brian calls A.J. "Mr. Talkative" because he is always talking on the telephone to his family. He's a great storyteller and loves to chat to just about anybody. He could tell stories all day long, even when the other guys are really tired and aren't quite up to hearing another A.J. tale. A.J. loves talking so much that he will even try to tell the guys stories about things that happened when they were with him! Must be like watching reruns.

Does A.J. have any bad habits? A.J. bites his nails and the skin around his fingers. He has tried everything to stop doing it, but he just can't. So it is no surprise that the thing he likes least about his looks is his fingers.

When A.J. was born, his great-grandmother knitted him a "blankey," as he called it, which soon became his favorite. He had it for fifteen years, but once when he was staying at a hotel in South Carolina, a maid threw it away, because by then the blankey wasn't looking too good. A.J. never got it back, which still bums him out, even though he knew that he was getting too old for a blanket. To this day, he twists his clothes nervously, like he did with his blankey long ago—he's got the holes in his clothes to prove it!

A.J. still doesn't have his driver's license . . . what's the deal? Since he is on the road so much, he hasn't had a chance to go back to take the written test again.

Other secrets about A.J.: He still gets nervous before beginning each new song while they are onstage. When he is on the road, A.J. brings a travel diary with him but doesn't write in it much. He is also a skilled puppeteer.

Love Life Sitch

When it comes to love and women, A.J. is a true romantic. A.J. says, "I'm the type of guy who likes to be there 24/7. I'm Mr. Roses." A.J. became a ladies' man at a young age. Once when he was fourteen, he went to a dance and kissed several different girls in one night! Even in eighth grade, A.J. was irresistible.

When A.J. was thirteen, he dated a girl named Christie. Sadly, Christie died in a car accident soon after that. Later, A.J. started to like a girl named Jennifer, but she dissed him by kissing someone else, supposedly because she thought A.J. was boring (!). A.J. is currently best friends with one of his exes, Marissa—they talk on the phone all the time.

A.J. believes in old-fashioned love and thinks it is important to be a gentleman to members of the opposite sex, which is something he learned from his mom, Denise. No matter how flirtatious he can be, respect always comes first.

A.J. is attracted to girls who are independent and confident. Other important attributes for the girl of his dreams: sensitivity and a sense of humor. When it comes down to it, he wants a girl who will stick with him through good times and bad, and someone for whom he can write his own brand of romantic poetry!

A description of his perfect night at home is also filled with swoon-worthy romance: a cold winter's eve, a fire in the fireplace, two mugs of hot chocolate with marshmallows, some mellow CDs playing, the lights dimmed inside with the moon shining brightly outside ... maybe wearing a pair of silk pajamas (though his favorite pair was lost in his luggage not too long ago). Since Mr. Romantic prefers hugs to kisses, his perfect night might end with some sweet cuddling while watching the movie *Ghost*. He says the story and especially the music really make him cry.

A.J.'s current romantic sitch: single and dating.

Future Holdings

What does A.J. think about 1998? "I think 1998 will be our biggest year yet!" he exclaims. He is thrilled when more and more fans come to the BSB shows—it makes him and the Boys very pleased.

A.J. definitely has a positive, can-do attitude when it comes to life. He likes to try new things, not only to have a whole bunch of different experiences, but also because he never wants to have any regrets when he is older. He wants to be able to look back on his life and say that he lived it to its fullest. Many would say he has done that already, having traveled all over the world, become an internationally known performer, met some of the world's hottest celebs, and gotten to do what he loves.

More 411 on A.J.

Favorite color: Yellow (as in the color of the Golden Arches)

Favorite food: McDonald's Double Quarter Pounder with cheese, large french fries, large Coke, large iced tea (no lemon)

Favorite junk food: Hershey's Cookies and Cream bar

Favorite drink: Mountain Dew

Favorite sport: Billiards—he's been playing since he was six years old (since he is not really into sports per se)

Hobbies: Movies (especially horror flicks), shopping, writing music and poetry, playing bass guitar, drawing cartoons

Instruments: Bass guitar, keyboards, saxophone

Favorite music: Dru Hill, Jamiroquai, Maxwell, Mark Morrisson, Boyz II Men, rap, R&B, hip-hop

Favorite movie: *Pulp Fiction* (he can recite all the lines!) and any kind of horror movie

Favorite actress: Geena Davis

Dream women: Cindy Crawford and Pamela Lee

Favorite actor: Dustin Hoffman

Hero: A.J.'s uncle, who played bass in a band called Richie and the Rockets in the 1950s; "He was a big influence on me even though they never made it big"

Favorite TV show: *Seinfeld*

Favorite cologne: CK One

Accessories: Big-hooped silver earrings in both ears, rings on almost all of his fingers, lots of chains (which he wears both around his neck and on his wrists), and of course, his signature sunglasses. (During a press conference while the Boys were in Malaysia, A.J. said if anyone ever caught him *sans* sunglasses, he would give that person a hundred bucks!)

Favorite school subject: English

What he looks for in a girl: He says the first thing he looks at is eyes, because he thinks it is important to be able to look deeply into someone's eyes and try to see into the person's soul; he also likes long hair more than short hair, but it doesn't matter to him if a girl is tall or short, fat or skinny

First job: Playing Dopey in *Snow White* in grade school

Real job: A.J. was working the trams as a tour guide for Universal Studios, Florida, before joining BSB

Odd fact: A.J. is a puppeteer

Favorite saying: "It's going to be funky!"

What he would have been if not in BSB: A dancer

CHAPTER 7

Howie "Howie D." Dorough: The Peacemaker

Vital Stats

Full name: Howard Dwaine Dorough
Hair: Black
Eyes: Brown
Height: 5'7"
Weight: 138 lbs.
Shoe size: 8
Nicknames: Howie D., Sweet D., Latin Lover
Birthplace: Orlando, Florida
Residence: Orlando, Florida
Birth date: August 22, 1973
Astrological sign: Leo
Marital status: Single
Family status: Parents Hoke and Paula; brother John; sisters Pollyanna, Caroline, and Angie (Howie is the youngest)
Pets: Christopher, a dog, and Oscar, a cat

Roots

Howie was the fifth and youngest child born to Hoke and Paula Dorough. Howie has four much older siblings, one brother and three sisters. Even though there is a big age difference between Howie and the rest of his sibs, the Dorough family is very close.

The Doroughs first knew they had a big talent on their hands when their youngest son, Howie, who was only three, jumped onto his grandma's bed and started singing the old song "Baby Face." But it wasn't until Howie was about seven years old that he got his more formal introduction to the world of entertainment by his sister, Pollyanna, who was eleven at the time. She was making the rounds doing local productions of plays and brought her baby brother along. His first gig was as a Munchkin in *The Wizard of Oz*, while his sister played Glinda, the Good Witch. Since he very much enjoyed his first stage experience, Howie later joined a choir and started doing more plays and musicals for a community theater, appearing in productions of *The Sound of Music*, *Showboat*, and *Camelot*.

Living in Orlando proved to be very lucky for Howie, because Disney's studios were also there. As a result, Howie got asked to be in a commercial for Disney World and landed small roles in two Disney feature films, *Parenthood* with Steve Martin and *Cop and a Half* with Burt Reynolds.

Howie was also in the original pilot for a Nickelodeon show called *Welcome Freshman*. He was part of the group cast from Orlando. After the pilot for the show was finished, the producers evaluated it and decided to cut the entire first cast. Then they hired all new cast members and the show became a hit. Howie was one of the actors who made it to the final callback, but unfortunately he didn't get the part in the new cast. It was something that upset him for a while, especially since he got so close to making it onto the show.

So by the time he got his big (biggest!) break with the Backstreet Boys, Howie had learned the importance of being able to survive rejection, which happens more often than not in the world of showbiz. Acceptance and success are rare, so he believes that you have to believe in yourself and keep on aiming for what you want.

During this time, Howie was also singing in church and taking voice lessons. It was through his voice teacher that he first met A.J.

His grandmother, Corene Wright, who was there at the very beginning of Howie's singing career (since it was her bed on which Howie jumped to sing his first solo), died in 1997, right before BSB became a huge hit in the States and their first CD was released here, which is something Howie is sad about. However, he said his grandma always knew he would make something of himself, so he feels great about proving her prediction right.

Up Close and Personal

Howie D. considers himself to be caring, respectful, and honest. The other Boys would agree; these are the qualities that have earned Howie the rep as the peacemaker or diplomat of the group. Brian calls Howie "Mr. Quiet," because if the Boys ever have disagreements (which are usually about minor things such as what the Boys are going to wear, where they are going, and so on), Howie sits back quietly and takes it all in. After hearing all the sides, he thinks about it a bit, forms his opinion, and then tells everyone what he believes is the fair thing to do. Even if they ask him for his opinion, he won't say so right away until he has carefully considered everyone's point of view.

Howie explains that his motto is "Do unto others as you would have them do unto you." He always tries to be very respectful and would never harsh on someone or dis them, because his feeling is that he wouldn't want to be treated that way himself.

In keeping with that motto, Howie has always been a person who is generous with his time, spirit, and resources—which is one of the reasons Howie is known by friends and family as "Sweet D." He has always been and continues to be involved with charities and helping others. When he was in high school he was part of a peer-counseling group called Friends, which encouraged kids to live a clean, drug-free life and to stay in school. When they first started, BSB helped out the Ronald McDonald House charity along with Whitney Houston and then got involved with SADD, Students Against Destructive Decisions.

Howie seems to be the sentimental one of the group, and he likes to keep video diaries of the Boys' shoots and tours. There are probably a lot of fans who would like to get their hands on those pieces of film!

The group unanimously votes Howie the neatest of the bunch. Since he is so careful with his stuff, it really bugs him when the airlines lose his luggage, which for some reason seems to happen to him more often than to any other BSBer.

Nick observes that Howie is always playing against the current fashion trends—he is always trying to be different. If tight pants are in, then Nick says Howie is into baggy pants, and vice versa.

When it comes to down time, Howie is not big into sitting around doing nothing, which he considers to be a waste of time. If he is away from home on tour, he finds calling his family is the most relaxing thing he can do. Whenever he is on tour, he writes several post-cards to his family and is sure to fill his suitcase with souvenirs and presents to bring back to them.

Howie, who is a professionally trained dancer, is a club kid to the Nth degree—he loves to go out club-bing and show off his dance moves whenever he gets the chance. He is also the guy in the group who can make his voice go the highest, so he is the one you hear singing the really high falsettos in BSB's songs.

Recently Howie has been teaching himself how to play guitar. He has also gotten some on-the-spot lessons from some of the musicians who play for BSB, including a guitarist who was on the road with them on a recent British tour. Howie is learning guitar now because it is something he has always wanted to do, but couldn't manage before because he was concentrating on his singing. The other Boys are really impressed with Howie's progress and are proud of his dedication to practicing. Apparently Howie takes out his guitar to play every chance he gets!

It was at Howie's suggestion that the Backstreet Boys recorded two of their songs—"Anywhere For You" and "I'll Never Break Your Heart"—in Spanish. Even though Howie grew up speaking English, he later started to learn Spanish (since he is half Puerto Rican) and gained a deep appreciation for the language. He also thought that having their songs in Spanish would help broaden their appeal to fans who speak Spanish as a first language or who live in predominantly Spanish-speaking countries. This is one of the reasons why Howie counts Jon Secada, who is a bilingual performer, as one of his favorites.

Secret Scoop

A.J. reveals that Howie has a thing about his hair, because it is so curly. So the Boys like to wind him up by messing with Howie D.'s hair whenever they get the chance, especially when Howie is on a big date.

Kevin explains that the reason one of Howie's nicknames is "Sweet D." is not because he loves chocolate cake, but because he is really thoughtful about others. Because Howie is half Puerto Rican (the other half is Irish), sometimes people call him "Latin Lover." But really, Howie is more of an old-fashioned romantic.

It seems that Howie never wants to eat another

Gummi Bear. What's the deal with that? Well, apparently once Howie said he liked them, and then fans started sending him tons of Gummi Bears, so naturally he ate them everyday. He eventually got so sick of them that he has stopped eating them—and chocolate too—because he is trying to watch his weight.

Some more revealing secrets about Howie D.: Howie is known to always do his push-ups and sit-ups before bed—now that's discipline! His favorite fairy tale is Beauty and the Beast. He really hates bugs and is actually kind of afraid of them.

Love Life Sitch

Howie's first real date was when he was fourteen. The lucky girl was in a play with Howie at the time—that's how they met. She was an "older woman"—by one year—but since neither of them was old enough to drive and even then Howie knew it would be uncool to pick her up on his bike, her mom drove. He doesn't remember taking a long time to prepare for the date, but he did put on way too much cologne, because he was trying to smell his very best.

When Howie turned eighteen, the girl he was dating at the time asked her parents for the house so she could throw a surprise party for Howie and his friends. Since Howie is so sweet himself, he appreciates it when others do nice and thoughtful things like that for him.

Howie is quite the romantic. For one date he pulled out all the stops, cooking the lucky girl a delicious dinner of grilled steaks, strawberries, and sparkling apple juice, which they ate by candlelight. Afterward the two drove out to the nearby airport, opened the sunroof, and watched as the planes flew over them. And once when Howie was in Germany, he even took a date to see the musical *Miss Saigon*—but it was performed in German, so he didn't understand a word of the play.

Howie D. has written love songs for girls and usually sings them to the girl who is the object of his affection. Once on a date he and his girl were walking along the beach and he began singing a song that he had written just for her. That must've tipped the romantic scales way over!

Unfortunately, while Howie can be a big sweetie, he has been the victim of a broken heart more than once. Sadly, two previous relationships ended because of the strain that traveling so much put on the relationship. Long-distance love can be very difficult and painful. Sometimes, especially with a schedule like Howie's, it is almost impossible. But good reasons don't make breaking up any easier. Even though Howie understood and respected the girls' honesty, he was really down and hurt when he and his girlfriends split up.

Howie D. is currently single. What kind of girl is he looking for? "I like someone who is always looking at things in a positive way," he says. "Someone who knows what she wants in life and [how] to go about getting it." He likes blondes but says that intelligence, a sense of humor, and all-around goodness are higher on his list. He is looking for a girl who "loves me for what I am—and can put up with my career," he told the *Orlando Sentinel*.

Howie also thinks sincerity is very important—both in the girl he is dating and in himself. If he doesn't have genuine feelings for a girl, he won't just say some stuff that he doesn't mean. Always the upstanding citizen, Howie has never two-timed a girl. He isn't shy about crying, either, because he considers it a natural expression of emotion.

Howie would consider himself to be a good kisser—at least that is what he has been told. How did he get to be so good? Like with anything else: Practice makes perfect! Howie digs hugging a lot, probably because he has such a big family and they are always hugging and kissing each other. But he especially likes it when a girl he is with hugs him—that's very special to him.

Howie might want to spend his next dream date sitting on a balcony on a snowy day, cuddling under some fur jackets and a warm blanket. Better have some warm socks, too!

Future Holdings

Howie's hopes for 1998? To spend more time at Disney World, his favorite place—even though he has been there about a billion times! Since he loves all kinds of foreign and exotic food, he especially likes to hit Epcot Center and sample all the different dishes.

More 411 on Howie D.

Favorite color: Purple

Favorite foods: All kinds of Asian food and many foreign foods; Mom's home cooking

Favorite drinks: Iced tea and Sprite

Favorite sports: Swimming, racketball, surfing, weight lifting, water skiing

Favorite things: His BSB necklace and a cross his mother gave him

Hobbies: Going clubbing and dancing, working out, movies, and hanging out with his Boys

Instrument: Guitar

Favorite music: Prince (The Artist Formerly Known As ...), Jon Secada (who is a major musical influence for him as well), Celine Dion, Bobby Brown, Michael Jackson, Al B. Sure, Phillip Bailey, soul and R&B music

Favorite movies: *The Outsiders* and *Willy Wonka and the Chocolate Factory*

Favorite actress: Demi Moore

Dream women: Salma Hayek, Cindy Crawford, and Brooke Shields

Favorite actor: Tom Hanks

Favorite book: *The Firm*, by John Grisham

His hero: His mom, who has supported him from the very beginning

Favorite TV show: *The Fresh Prince of Bel-Air*

Accessories: Silver bracelets, earring on left ear, silver chains

Favorite colognes: Cool Water and CK One

Favorite school subject: Math

What he looks for in a girl: Having a positive attitude; being supportive, upbeat, and ambitious

Favorite saying: "Cheers"

He's most likely to: Because Howie is such a romantic, don't be surprised if he asks you to take a moonlit walk along the beach!

What he thought he'd be: A police officer

Favorite item of clothing: His vests—he has forty at home, all different styles and colors, new ones and old-fashioned ones, but his favorite of these is one that is red-and-mustard-colored

Favorite toy: As a kid, his favorite toy was a Batman motorcycle that he could really ride, and not only did Howie ride the heck out of that thing, he also could do wheelies on it (not without a few wipe-outs, of course!)

Favorite pizza toppings: Pepperoni and mushrooms, though when he's at Pizza Hut, he always orders the Supreme

Favorite time of the year: Christmastime, because people are so nice to each other during that time of year, and because he enjoys trimming the tree and going to holiday parties

CHAPTER 8

Nick Carter: The Youngest Boy on the Block

Vital Stats

Full name: Nicholas Gene Carter
Hair: Blond
Eyes: Blue
Height: about 6'—and still growing!
Weight: 162 lbs.
Shoe size: 11
Nicknames: Prefers Nick; Nicky, Hyperman, Kaos, Messy
    Marvin (he's always spilling stuff!)
Birthplace: Jamestown, New York
Birth date: January 28, 1980
Astrological sign: Aquarius
Marital status: Single
Family status: Parents Jane and Bob; brother Aaron;
        sisters B.J. (Bobbie Jean), Lesley, and Angel; Nick is
        the oldest of five children—Aaron and Angel are
        fraternal twins and the youngest
Pets: Simba, a Golden Retriever; Bandit, Muffy, and Blue
    Boy—cats

Roots

Nick is not the only celebrity who was born in the hospital in Jamestown, New York: Lucille Ball, the famous comedienne and actress, was also born there, albeit several years before Nick. Nick loved growing up in his family's house on Webber Road in Jamestown. Out of the five Carter kids, only Nick and his sis B.J. were born in Jamestown; his other three siblings were born after the family moved to Florida.

Nick's grandparents also lived in the same town. His grandfather and father owned a small lounge called the Yankee Rebel. His dad would DJ and choose what music they played at the lounge. Even when little Nicky was in diapers, he used to dance around the dance floor. He has pictures of himself as a toddler with huge headphones on, dancing around. Since he was what he calls "a little chunk," his family called him "Charlie Brown" back then.

Besides his love for music and dancing, his love for video games also began at a very young age. One time his family thought they lost little "Nicky," as they called him. They looked all over for him and eventually found him sitting on a stool in the lounge playing a game of Pac-Man—wearing a diaper!

Eventually, his folks decided they wanted a change of pace and thought Florida would be a great place to make a new start. So when Nick was about five or six years old, his parents packed their stuff into a trailer and put the family in their Cadillac Eldorado and headed south.

Since Nick's father was working at a retirement

home, the family lived there for about a year. Nick and his sister B.J. used to play with frogs in the mud around where they lived. They have a picture of the two of them covered in mud, with frogs on their heads!

A year or two after they got to Florida, Nick started to become truly interested in performing—singing, dancing, whatever he could do in front of an audience or a camera. Soon thereafter he got the lead role in his school's production of *The Phantom of the Opera.* Later, he was a featured vocalist in the pre-game shows for the Tampa Bay Buccaneers football team for their 1991 and 1992 seasons. By the time he was twelve, he had performed in and won the 1992 New Original Amateur Hour and was already in TV commercials for the Florida State Lottery and The Money Store. To join BSB, both Nick and A.J. turned down offers to be in the Mickey Mouse Club.

When Nick first became a member of BSB, he hadn't yet finished school, but he couldn't stay in his regular school because he had to be on the move and have a more flexible schedule. So he did something called "home school," which meant that he still had to do all of his homework and study all of the same things that were taught in his regular school—which he did, while he was on tour! He had his own teacher, with whom he would spend two hours a day. This teacher gave him his exams, too. His dad, who often went with Nick and the Boys on tour, kept an eye on his fair-haired son to make sure his school work always got done. No special treatment for the singing star!

Nick is very close to his family and misses them a lot when he is away on tour, which is often. He especially misses his younger siblings, for whom he used to baby-sit quite often, since he was the oldest Carter kid. He tries to visit them in their thirteen-room Orlando mansion whenever he can. The family itself is very tightly knit and they all watch out for one another.

And it seems Nick is not the only singing Carter. His younger brother Aaron, the twin of sister Angel, has a single out called "Crush On You," which has become a hit on some international charts.

Up Close and Personal

When Nick first became a member of the Backstreet Boys, he was very young (only thirteen years old), so he has matured and grown up quite a bit over the five-year span of their career. While he admits he has learned a lot—both from being in a fast-paced business and just by going through normal teenage growing pains—he still feels like he can be a kid when he wants to be. His family and friends at home probably notice the changes in Nick more since they see him only briefly with very long intervals in between. They think that Nick is handling his fame very maturely, but they also let him be who he wants to be.

Being the youngest but growing up quickly allows Nick to be like almost two different people when he needs to. He can be responsible and practical when he is around people who are older than him, such as the record company people or the press. But he can also relax when he is with people his own age and just be himself.

Even though Nick is the youngest BSBer, he gets equal say. All the Boys make the decisions together, from what song they want to release next to what their next projects will be. They are totally supportive of each other, like a family. The older Boys give Nick advice when he asks, especially since they have been through some experiences different from his own. He has the best of both worlds in a way: He may be the youngest group member, but he is the oldest sibling in his own real family. He likes having four older "brothers" to help him out along the way.

Nick does do some of the songwriting, but mostly in collaboration with the other Boys. About five years ago, Nick started taking drum lessons and has gotten quite good. Now he plays a bit onstage during their shows, sometimes with Kevin, who plays the piano.

Nick loves to spend time at home with his folks and sibs, eating lots of food and playing computer games, especially Nintendo. He enjoys watching movies like *I Love Trouble* with Julia Roberts, but he is not big into romantic flicks. He also likes to shoot hoops with his friends and rollerblade. When he and the guys are on the road—especially during the long hours they spend traveling from place to place—Nick loves to draw comics and cartoons of the other Boys.

Nick thinks of himself as an ordinary, down-to-earth guy and hopes that any girl he ends up with wouldn't need more than that. He loves getting hugs, though, whether from his fans or the other Boys. Nick admits to being able to cry, but he tries not to in front of people other than his family or the guys. He does believe it is possible to be friends with girls, and likes to make friends with girls when he travels on tour—that way he can call them again to talk when he returns to those countries or cities.

The other Boys consider Nick to be the most hyper and clumsiest of the crew, which has earned him his nicknames of "Hyperman," "Kaos," and "Messy Marvin" (because he often spills stuff all over the place). But he is also very carefree, which is a trait that Kevin envies. But a combination of his laid-back attitude and youth can sometimes keep Nick from being serious and getting down to business when he needs to. Howie agrees that Nick has a lot of energy but doesn't always know how to focus it.

Brian considers Nick the little brother he never had. He likes to teach Nick things, and thinks that Nick has grown up a lot in a short period of time and is mature for his age. However, sometimes Nick can take his basketball playing too seriously and, according to Brian, gets very frustrated.

Nick sometimes competes with A.J. for being the prankster of the group. During one of their recent tours, Nick hid a sock filled with different stinky stuff (no one will say what . . .) behind the drums so that during the show the stuffed sock really started to smell and no one but Nick knew what it was. He also once gave their manager Donna Wright some gum that tasted like fish. Another time, Sneaky Nicky stole all of A.J.'s clothes from his hotel room one night. (Considering how much A.J. loves clothes, he probably was not too psyched to see all of his clothes gone when he woke up the next morning!)

But the Boys have not taken Nick's pranks lying down. To get their revenge, they once pushed Nick out of their dressing room in front of a bunch of girls who were outside. In and of itself, that is not such a harsh joke, but Nick was in his underwear at the time, so you can imagine his embarrassment (and the surprise of his fans!).

Nick has a rep for being the cute one of the Backstreet Boys, which is a name he doesn't mind. However, being the youngest doesn't win him special treatment—all the Boys treat each other the same, respectfully and fairly.

How does Nick handle being a pin-up poster boy? He says that at first it was kind of weird, but he has grown used to it and likes it. It's flattering and satisfying for him to know that girls like him and his music, but being the modest guy that he is, sometimes he wonders what all the fuss over him is about. . . .

Secret Scoop

Nick confesses to not having many friends, except the other four Boys. He also says he wasn't popular in school because he knew he was different from everyone else and was driven at an early age to pursue his music career. The case might actually be that since he spent most of his high-school years with the band and took his lessons from a tutor, he never got the chance to socialize with his schoolmates. If Nick had been in school full-time, his friend situation would most certainly have been very different.

What Nick might not confess is that he listens to country music. But, then again, he listens to all types of music. One interviewer found the following CDs in Nick's CD case: AC/DC, Bone Thugs 'N' Harmony, Oasis, Kriss Kross, Prince, Tom Petty, R. Kelly, Jodeci, N-Trance, Lenny Kravitz, Mary J. Blige, and Nirvana.

Nick once had a little part in *Edward Scissorhands* with Johnny Depp in 1990. But if you are going to rent the movie just to see Nick in a big feature film, you might want to save your four bucks. He can be seen for like a second—he is the little blond boy who runs across a lawn. Not exactly Oscar material, but he was quite young then and this was many years before BSB came into being, so give the guy a break.

Nick used to be afraid of flying. He is no longer that fearful of it (especially since he has to do it so much), but he still really does not like to fly. How does he cope? He tries to sleep during as much of the flight as he can.

Though he is the youngest, Nick has the biggest feet of any guy in the group. He grew tall very quickly. By the time he was sixteen, he was already six feet tall!

When Nick was asked to rate himself on the cute-meter from one to ten, Nick modestly rated himself about a seven and a half, give or take. What does Nick consider to be his least cute body part? His ears! He says that they are too big and stick out too far.

Nick has practically grown up in front of one kind

© Paul Bergen/Redferns/Retna Ltd.

Backstreet is
MORE than
BACK!

Getting in a little practice
before the big show.

© Paul Bergen/Redferns/Retna Ltd.

Jokester B-Rok hamming for the camera!

A.J. singing to his fans at a
London concert in late 1996.

A sultry, smokin' Kevin strikes a pose to die for! He sure has come a long way from his log cabin days. . . .

© Mick Hutson/Redferns/Retna Ltd.

The "Onstage Boys" givin' their fans their all.

© Ernie Panicciolli/Retna Ltd.

Nick having fun at New York City's Motown Cafe. The Backstreet Boys were there to give a private performance for WKTU radio contest winners.

The Big Day at last! On August 12, 1997, the Boys held a press conference at the All-Star Café in Times Square in New York City to launch their debut album in the States.

Howie "Sweet D." Dorough singing a sweet tune.

© Janet Macoska/Retna Ltd.

A.J. and his mom, Denise, spending some quality time on one of BSB's 1997 U.S. tours. Denise McLean accompanies the Boys on many of their tours, including those to several of the foreign countries they've visited.

© Michael Linssen/Redferns/Retna Ltd.

BSB fans show their Backstreet pride at a concert. This fan must be sweet on Nick!

© Alain Benainous/Gamma Liaison

Congratulations—again! BSB scoops the Viewer's Select Award at the 1997 MTV Europe Awards in Rotterdam—for the second year in a row!

Check out the Boys in leather at the *Billboard* Awards in 1997—
they were there to present an award.

of camera or another. He didn't always feel comfortable in front of the camera, he says. But over time, he has gotten more used to it and does what feels natural to him.

When asked to which Spice Girl he would most likely send a big bouquet of flowers, Nick answered, "Emma. Now she's really cute!"

Believe it or not, Nick can be grumpy in the mornings. But his worst offense, says Howie, is that he hogs the Nintendo. Nick admits that he does hog the Nintendo, but there is a good reason for it. When they are on tour, the Boys often have to stay put in the hotel, so Nick can't go outside to shoot hoops (which is what he'd rather be doing). So, to pass the time, relax, and even escape to another world, he plays a lot of Nintendo. Makes sense!

Love Life Sitch

So what's up in Nick's love life? You would think he has had a million girlfriends by now, being so talented, handsome, internationally famous, and all. Millions of fans have it bad for Nick. He gets hundreds of love letters from female fans every week. Once, when the Boys were onstage in Germany, a fan held up a sign that said, "Nick, I want to have your baby!" Not the most subtle or romantic proposal in the world, but the Boys must have gotten lots of mileage winding up Nick with that one. Nick admits that he WOULD DEFINITELY date a fan.

Even though Nick gets so much attention all the

time, in reality he can be quite shy and sensitive. In interviews, he often keeps himself in the background. When he likes someone, he gets really quiet around her—and almost ignores her! Sometimes, if he gets too close to the object of his affection, he not only clams up, he gets a tingly/queasy feeling in his stomach, too.

Nick likes older girls and girls who are smaller than him (who must be easy to find, considering he is more than six feet tall!). Other qualities he looks for: very pretty, long dark hair, honest, loyal, romantic. But probably most importantly, Nick wants to be with a girl who likes/loves him for who he is deep down rather than for how he looks or how popular he is. He wouldn't take receiving flowers from a young woman as an insult to his manliness, however—he's a '90s kind of guy!

Nick is single and he does date. But since he and the Boys are always traveling and touring, he is never in one place long enough to get close to any one girl. When he does get the chance to go out with a girl on a date, he likes to make the most of the short time they have together and just have fun. What would Nick do on a dream date? He might take a trip with his honey-to-be down to the Florida Keys to do some serious scuba diving. Don't forget your bathing suit!

Future Holdings

For the present and near future, Nick is thrilled to be a member of the Backstreet Boys, especially now that they are enjoying their much-deserved success at home in the States. Although he might like to go to college someday, it isn't really in the cards right now, since there is little time for studying. If he did attend school, Nick would like to major in Art. He has no immediate plans to move out of his family's house, especially since he is never there to begin with! It doesn't hurt having someone to take care of the cleaning and clothes washing, since that is *not* Nick's biggest interest.

He also loves drawing cartoons, though he doesn't get a whole lot of time to devote to that. He has a ton of ideas and someday soon hopes to get the chance to work on them, maybe even with someone else.

If Nick was going to act in a movie, he would prefer to land a role in an action movie, perhaps something similar to *Mortal Kombat*, or a war movie. He would also like to direct and produce an action movie someday.

More 411 on Nick

Favorite color: Dark green

Favorite foods: Pizza ("Hold the anchovies!"), McDonald's

Favorite drink: Coca-Cola

Favorite sports: Basketball, boating, fishing; he is a certified scuba diver and loves to drive his family's boat in the Gulf of Mexico

Hobbies: Drawing, collecting football cards, playing video games

Greatest fear: The dark

Instrument: Drums

Favorite cars: Stingrays and Camaros

Favorite holiday: Halloween

Favorite music: Journey (during concerts, Nick usually sings his favorite Journey songs like "Open Arms"), Nirvana, Jodeci, Oasis, Shai, Michael Jackson

Favorite movie: *Aliens*

Favorite actresses: Christina Ricci, Sigourney Weaver

Dream women: Jewel, Cindy Crawford, Sharon Stone

Favorite actor: Bruce Willis

Hero: Film director Ridley Scott

Favorite TV shows: *The X-Files, The Fresh Prince of Bel-Air, Beavis & Butt-head, Mad About You*

Favorite cologne: Gravity

Least favorite school subject: Algebra

Biggest indulgence: He loves to buy sneakers and gold jewelry (he doesn't wear earrings)

What he looks for in a girl: Nick says he prefers brown-haired girls, but "it doesn't really matter to me as long as they have a good personality and they're really nice"

Dream date: A walk on the beach with a kind-hearted girl

He's most likely to: Draw your picture. He is rarely seen without a pencil in hand

First jobs: The lead in his fourth grade production of *The Phantom of the Opera.* Nick also appeared in commercials for the Florida State Lottery and The Money Store. He was also the featured vocalist for the Tampa Bay Buccaneers' pre-game show for two years

Favorite saying: "It's all good!"

CHAPTER 9

Brian "B-Rok" Littrell: The Joker

Vital Stats

Full name: Brian Thomas Littrell
Hair: Chestnut brown (though it's sometimes blond; it's
    not naturally curly, except for the curls in front)
Eyes: Blue
Height: 5'8"
Weight: 145 lbs.
Shoe size: 10
Nicknames: B-Rok, Seaver, Mr. Joker
Birthplace: Lexington, Kentucky
Residence: Orlando, Florida (an apartment near Universal
    Studios, which he shares with Kevin and Howie)
Birth date: February 20, 1975
Astrological sign: Pisces
Marital status: Single
Family status: Parents Jackie and Harold; an older brother,
    Harold junior; Brian and fellow BSBer Kevin
    Richardson are cousins
Pets: Missy, a cat

Roots

Brian Thomas Littrell was born on February 20, 1975, in St. Joseph Hospital, the second son for parents Jackie and Harold. Harold Littrell worked for IBM, where he had worked ever since he was eighteen years old. He had also spent four years in the navy but met Brian's mother right before he shipped out. Brian's brother is three years older than Brian, which seemed like a bigger age difference when the two boys were young.

When Brian was only five years old, he was diagnosed with a staph infection (a disease of the blood and heart), partially because he was born with a hole in his heart and had a heart murmur—but his family didn't know that until he got sick. He had been riding his Big Wheel when it flipped over and he skinned his knee. Normally that wouldn't have been a big deal, because he was not really hurt, but a couple of weeks later, when the family was at his grandfather's house, Brian slipped, fell, and hit his head pretty badly. His parents took him to the hospital because they were worried he might have a concussion. That accident turned out to be very lucky, because it was at the hospital that they discovered he had 'this very serious, even deadly infection, which had set in two weeks earlier when he had scraped his knee. He ended up staying in the hospital for two months because he was very weak and sick from the infection.

At the time, his prognosis was very bad. His doctors believed he had no chance of surviving his illness; they even told his parents to start making funeral arrangements! His mother was totally distraught by this news and prayed in church for her son's recovery. Eventually the infection started to clear up and then completely went away! Brian and his family thanked God for this miracle.

It took some time for Brian to get back on his feet and do the things that most healthy, vigorous five-year-olds do, but once he did, he never stopped. He started to play some soccer, because he loved to be able to run around, especially since he knew what it was like to be stuck in a hospital (for a five-year-old, two months is a very long time!). His parents, however, were still worried about Brian's weak heart and didn't want him to overdo it. Eventually, though, he started to play basketball in a church league, which he still loves to play to this day.

Religion always played a part in the Littrell family's life, and because of that, they also had an appreciation for music. Both of his parents loved to sing in their Baptist church choir. Brian had to spend many Sundays at church. But then Brian also joined the choir and discovered his own love for music and his talent for singing. He had his first solo in front of a congregation of fifteen hundred people when he was only six or seven years old. Later, he was often asked to sing in other churches in his region or at weddings. Along with his older cousin Kevin, to whom Brian was very close, he would sing at family gatherings. They loved to perform standards from barbershop quartets, fifties-style doo-wop, and contemporary hits.

As Brian grew a little older, he also found a love for pop music and spent a lot of time listening to

Top 40 and urban radio stations to hear his favorite artists such as MC Hammer and Boyz II Men. He then became more familiar with the smooth sounds of R&B singers and especially came to admire Luther Vandross, whom he now counts as one of his influences.

When Brian was in high school he got the call from cousin Kev to come down to Florida to audition for a new boy singing group. Up until that point, he had never really considered singing professionally, especially since his only performing experience had been singing in church choirs. But luckily for BSB fans everywhere, Brian (soon to be "B-Rok") Littrell had his eyes open and was able to recognize this once-in-a-lifetime opportunity. When he got down to Florida, Brian had a crash course in show business—and has never looked back.

Up Close and Personal

Brian would describe himself as being humorous and athletic. He could also add outgoing to the list, but he wasn't always that way. Being in the group has brought Brian out of his shell. He says that he used to be more timid about what he did, especially in public, but now that he is older (and, it might be added, world-famous), he is more relaxed and comfortable with himself.

Brian is a self-admitted clown. However, he also reveals that he is a deep person as well. The other guys back this up: Kevin says that Brian is a real clown, while A.J. reveals that Brian cries when he is happy, like when their album went gold. (Apparently so did Kevin! Talk about sensitive guys . . .)

Brian spends a lot of time thinking and talking about things. He wants people to see both sides of his personality because he doesn't want to come across only as someone who is clowning around. Onstage or with fans, he puts on his funny side, because "I want people to see the happy me, as that's what I am 99 percent of the time," he said in an interview for *Top of the Pops* magazine. To show the sensitive side of his nature, he tries to be very honest in interviews so the fans can see what he is all about.

So, what is he like that other 1 percent of the time, when he is not happy? He admits that there are days when, just like anyone else, he can be a real grouch if he wakes up on the wrong side of the bed or hasn't had enough sleep. How does he deal with the other Boys when he is like that? With honesty. He simply tells them that he is not in a good mood, and since they spend so much time together and know each other so well, they step off and leave him alone without taking it personally.

Brian likes being close to people and considers himself to be a warm guy. He has a healthy, laid-back attitude about those who "kiss and tell"—he knows that there are people who gossip and spin stories out there, but he doesn't let them bother him or stop him from doing what he wants to do. He doesn't think it is worth wasting time worrying or not enjoying himself for fear of people spreading gossip. He just lives his life.

One of the things he misses the most when he is on the road with the guys is his own bed. Brian has a king-size waterbed that he bought for $50 (he claims it was practically brand-new—what a bargain!), which he loves to sleep on when he is home. Often, thinking about his bed is the thing that makes him the most homesick. He loves coming home, jumping into bed, and sliding into his own sheets with his own pillows and blankets. That makes him feel like he is really home.

How does Brian spend a fun Friday night when he is home? Chilling with his three best friends, going to catch a movie, scarfing down a huge bucket of popcorn (which he *loves*), maybe going out for a dinner of steak, fries, and salad after the movie, meeting up with some other friends, meeting some pretty girls—Brian isn't picky. He just likes hanging.

Nick and Brian are very close. However, the two of them can be very competitive, especially when it comes to sports, particularly basketball, which is Brian's favorite. He and Nick shoot hoops whenever they can, but Nick doesn't like losing to Brian. Brian and Nick usually like to share a hotel room when they are touring—unfortunately, the group also deems Bri the messiest of the group, so it is not always easy to be his roommate.

Brian sometimes likes attention—and knows how to get it. If A.J. strikes up a conversation, Brian can steal the scene by jumping around, making funny faces like a monkey, and doing other silly things. Brian defends his comedic antics by saying that he gets his silly side from his family. He explains that they are always trying to make one another laugh or do funny things with one another. Sounds like a barrel of monkeys!

Brian is the other BSBer with a southern accent, which he gets teased for a lot when he is in Orlando, since most people who live there don't have any kind of specific accent. The Boys sometimes rag Brian about being a bit of a bumpkin, but they really don't think of him like that.

Brian knows that it is because of the group's fame that they receive special treatment and get to hang out with an elite group of celebrities and other famous people in fabulous clubs such as the chi-chi Sky Bar at the Mondrian Hotel in Los Angeles, but he and the other guys don't let it go to their heads. They can still be starstruck, like when Cindy Crawford walked past them at the bar and Howie could barely breathe. "But it *is* weird because you're an entertainer—you're put in that position and we know we're no different or better than anybody else," Brian says.

Secret Scoop

Brian claims not to have any deep, dark secrets, but he does have some things that he tries to keep private. "You need to keep something for yourself for your own sanity," he says.

Probably Brian's biggest confession—which is no longer a deep, dark secret—is that, like A.J., he bites his fingernails, which he has done his whole life. Even when he was young, his mother was always saying,

"Get your fingers out of your mouth!" but he still hasn't been able to break the habit. What is especially embarrassing for him is that when he signs autographs girls notice his fingers and say something to him about it, but he still does it. He is also afraid of heights.

Brian has two scars on his body that aren't often seen. One is on his lower stomach, which he got from having an appendectomy; the other is on his head, from when he had a confrontation with a table when he was twelve.

Brian doesn't have any tattoos but has said that he wants one. Where? On his upper back, between his shoulder blades. What would he get? Not a flower or something boring, that's for sure. He hasn't quite decided yet. . . .

According to the liner notes for the "I'll Never Break Your Heart" single, Brian says that the nickname "B-Rok" came from a basketball saying, "shoot some rocs." Hmm.

If Brian could be someone else, who would he be? He says Brad Pitt, because the actor is popular with the girls and very good-looking. He would also choose to be Tom Cruise (when Bri's hair is dark, some people have even said that he looks like the star).

Brian is a big Mariah Carey fan. In fact, once when he was in London, he waited in a car outside of Tower Records in Piccadilly Circus just to see what the pop diva looked like up close in the flesh.

Which *Friends* star would he go for, given a choice between Courteney Cox and Jennifer Aniston? He'd pick Jennifer—he says that both women are beautiful, but Jennifer is in a whole different league. He wouldn't mind landing a guest spot on their TV show or starring in a movie with both of them. His other female star picks: Pamela Lee over Sandra Bullock and Demi Moore over Gwyneth Paltrow.

Who is the BSBer most likely to get hitched first? The Boys put their money on Brian, but you never know. . . .

Love Life Sitch

When Brian was in high school, there was a girl he liked but she didn't like him back. She then went for another guy. Later she began to like him, but he decided he didn't like her anymore, because she didn't turn out to be the kind of person he thought she was.

Brian says that the two hardest things about being a famous music star are being away from home so much and not being able to have the time to get serious with a girl. He and the Boys barely have time to meet girls in any substantial way, much less go out on dates and develop meaningful relationships. He is not into one-night stands, because he is an old-fashioned romantic kind of guy. He wants to get to know a person before he even kisses her. Marriage is very important to him, but since he is young, he says, he isn't in a hurry to get hitched anytime soon.

What is the most important thing he is looking for in a girl? He very much wants someone who is her own person, who is independent and successful in her own right. It's not a turn-on for him to have girls be interested in him just because he is in the music

biz—they have to like him for who he is. "I find independence really sexy," he says.

Looks-wise, Brian prefers girls with blond or light
brown hair (though he also says hair color is not
that important), blue eyes, nice legs, and long nails.
Personality-wise, he likes girls who are intelligent, outgoing, have a good sense of humor, are determined,
and have a lot of energy (kind of like him).

When it comes to dating, Brian says that anyone he
dates has to be understanding of hectic touring schedules. He knows that most girls have a hard time dating
someone who is rarely around, so he'd rather work on
building a relationship when he is off the road for
longer periods of time. He says timing is very important because he believes finding love is all about being
in the right place at the right time.

What would be Brian's ideal way to spend a night
inside with his honey? If he had his choice, he'd be in
some cozy room that had a huge soft couch, cushions
all over the floor, and a big-screen TV. He would cook
a romantic dinner for two, and afterward they could
cuddle up on the big couch and watch a flick, maybe
While You Were Sleeping or *Sleepless in Seattle*
(that's the romantic side of him coming through loud
and clear). He might wear some cotton PJ bottoms
with a vest—and some soft socks to keep his feet
warm, of course!

If Brian were your boyfriend, what could he offer
you? "A little love, caring, understanding, and emotion," he says. He would even let you borrow his
clothes, because he thinks having a girlfriend wear his
clothes is romantic.

Brian says he is currently single and hasn't really had a girlfriend for a couple of years. He felt he had to break up with one girl because of his being in the group. There were rumors at one point that he had a secret girlfriend, but we'll leave that kind of speculation to the tabloids.

Future Holdings

What other things would Brian like to pursue in the future? He says acting is likely, especially since he is so at ease on TV even though he hasn't had any formal acting lessons. There is word that there is a Backstreet Boys movie in the works and that they want it to have a gothic-comic-book-like feel, based on the comic books that Nick is working on. If the movie does happen, not only Brian but also all the Boys will get their shot at acting! Brian also thinks it would be cool to be a VJ or star in a Jim Carrey flick.

Brian also would love to teach sports to kids in school, maybe even get a teaching degree in Phys Ed. He wouldn't even need to be paid, he says; he would just enjoy being involved with kids in high school.

He also would like to produce for other musical artists, write songs, and—on the nonshowbiz side— collect cars, which he would like to work on himself, if he ever had the time. (Doesn't look like he will have much leisure time anytime soon!)

Brian admits that some of the Boys have gotten offers to pursue solo careers, which is something they all would like to do someday, but they plan to stay together for the foreseeable future. They all have the same goals right now and want to achieve the same things, so it makes sense to stay together and move forward as a team. As Brian said in a *Top of the Pops* interview, "The main thing for us at the moment is to concentrate on getting this right. It's going to be a long time before we think about calling it quits."

More 411 on Brian

Favorite color: Midnight blue

Favorite foods: Mac and cheese; cheeze pizza (he loves cheese)

Favorite drink: Iced tea

Favorite sports: Basketball, weight lifting, water skiing, golf

Hobbies: Shopping, movies

Greatest fear: Heights

Instruments: Trumpet and percussion

Favorite music: Boyz II Men, Madonna, Mariah Carey, Bobby Brown, Luther Vandross, Take Six, Brian McKnight, Babyface

Favorite BSB song: "Don't Leave Me," " 'cause the track and the words are just slammin'!"

Favorite movie: *Trainspotting*

Favorite actress: Sandra Bullock

Dream women: Jada Pinkett, Pamela Lee

Favorite actors: Jim Carrey, Tom Hanks

Hero: Luther Vandross

Favorite TV show: *The Fresh Prince of Bel-Air*

Favorite colognes: Safari by Ralph Lauren, Photo by Lagerfeld

Accessories: Stud earrings and a silver chain with a big cross—but his favorite is a gold chain with a "B-Rok" pendant that he got when he was in Australia

What attracts him to girls: He is attracted most to a girl's eyes, but he likes somebody to whom having her own career is important and who treats him like a normal person; since Brian considers himself to be old-fashioned and respectful, he is looking for a girl who shares his values

Dream date: Picnic in the park

Favorite saying: "I guess"

PART THREE

Behind the Scenes
with the Boys

CHAPTER 10

Backstage Boys

It has been an amazing journey thus far for the Boys from Kentucky and Florida. They went from performing in church choirs and local talent shows to becoming the headlining performers at some of the biggest and most important music venues in the world. They have logged a lot of miles, both on the road and in the air, going back and forth between North America, Europe, Asia, and Australia. They have traveled to such far-off locales as Singapore, Malaysia, and Hong Kong. In the five years since BSB was formed, they have performed live in front of millions of fans. A.J., Howie, Kevin, Nick, and Brian have lived a lifetime worth of dreams at a very young age and in a very short time.

Besides racking up about a bazillion frequent-flier miles, the Boys have almost as many stories about what it has been like for them to be on the road for most of the past three years. From hilarious backstage antics to sharing a dressing room with the "spiciest" five women in the world, the past three years have been anything but boring.

So what's it like behind the scenes with the Boys? Read on for the inside scoop!

Does Playing Together Mean Staying Together?

It's amazing that, touring as much and as consistently as the Backstreet Boys do, they haven't yet killed each other! Actually, the Boys think of each other as brothers. The five of them consider themselves to be a family, especially since they are together so much—not quite 24/7/365, but pretty close. And when they are on tour, they are more like a family with *lots* of relatives, in the form of the crew, the band, tour managers, drivers, stylists, sound engineers, and everyone else. But the immediate family—the party of five—have a lot of fun together, confide in one another, and rely on each other as friends. Since the five of them are tight with their respective *real* immediate families, they bring their "family values," so to speak, to their relationships with each other.

How would they describe being together that much? It can get chaotic, they admit. Sometimes the constant togetherness can be grueling or even a little annoying, no matter how close they are. They are young guys with distinct personalities, so it is only natural that sometimes things can get a little hairy. So when BSB is on the road to everywhere (which is most of the time), they all follow certain rules to maintain their sanity and not get too sick of one another.

For instance, they try to give one another as much physical and mental space as possible. They do get along totally great with each other, but sticking to this rule allows all of them to feel like they can have some private time without always having to be one fifth of BSB every minute of every day.

The Boys say the most important key to getting along is verbal communication—meaning that they talk things out when somebody has a problem, rather than let tempers simmer and then perhaps explode, or hurt feelings fester and never get resolved. That's actually good advice for any family or group of friends. By now the Boys are quite used to one another's habits and moods, so things must go more smoothly than ever.

Every so often—as is only natural—they do have an argument about something, usually trivial, but they never, ever hit each other and they always make up really quickly. Since most of the guys are affectionate, they usually make up by giving each other a hug or maybe a kiss on the cheek. After that, all is forgiven and forgotten.

Taking a Ride on the Magic Bus

In the early days the Boys didn't have a lot of money, so they clocked many, many hours on tour buses, driving rather than flying from place to place. When people are in such close quarters for long periods of time, funny things are bound to happen. What would it be like to be on the Backstreet Boys tour bus?

Brian and A.J. are the messiest BSB members. A.J.

leaves food wrappers all over the place. But even though A.J. can be a bit of a Messy Marvin, he is very particular about his belongings and gets a little p.o.'d if he thinks someone has gone through his stuff.

All of the Boys have extra-big appetites when they are on the move, so it is important for them to keep their tour bus and hotel fridges stocked with all their favorite foods. Since A.J. tends to eat all of the food quickly, the other four Boys try to get their share of the food first. A.J. is also very territorial about his McDonald's french fries—he is definitely *not* into sharing those! Hands off! If Brian and Nick get to the food first, they tend to snag all the potato chips and candy bars. But not all of the Boys are junk-food junkies: Howie and Kevin are the health nuts of the group, so they tend to go for the healthier items.

Since the traveling, shows, and promotional appearances take their toll, the Boys make sure to get plenty of sleep so that they can keep up their energy and their health. Sometimes they have to sleep on the tour bus, especially if they have back-to-back stops and need to travel through the night to get to their next venue on time.

Brian claims that Nick is the sneakiest when it comes to picking the best bunk bed on the bus. Nick's secret? He tries to be the first one to the bus—even a couple of hours early, just to save the best bed for himself! After sleeping on the road so often, however, the Boys have pretty much figured out the sleeping arrangements by now: Howie prefers the back left bunk on the bottom, with A.J. above him and Kevin across from him. Brian and Nick like to choose bunks toward the end of the bus.

Even if they have worked out the sleeping configuration according to everyone's satisfaction, sleeping conditions on the bus are not always ideal. Nick complains that sometimes it can get cold on the bus, which makes it a bit uncomfortable for sleeping. Also, Nick says that some nights he wakes up several times and is often disoriented. When that happens, it takes a while for him to remember where he is. Nick reveals, too, that Howie sometimes snores, because he sleeps with his mouth open. Brian adds that every once in a while Howie talks in his sleep, but usually he mumbles, so they don't know what he is saying. Sometimes if the Boys try talking to him, Howie responds like he can understand them—but he goes right on sleeping!

So who drives the bus while the Boys are sound asleep in their cozy little bunk beds? A bus driver, of course. They had one driver named Conrad. Even though Conrad was from Germany, he spoke English pretty well. The Boys liked him because Conrad, whom they also called "Superboy," was pretty cool and would make pit stops at Mickey D's for them whenever they wanted (one of the fastest ways to the Boys' hearts). Conrad also didn't nag the guys, which was a good thing in their book.

Once, a couple of years ago when they were touring around the States, the Boys threw a Halloween party on their old tour bus (the same one Whitney Houston had used). They were able to have about twenty people at the bus party. The bus was decorated by

A.J.'s mother and the bus driver with fake cobwebs and other Halloween things.

But it is not all parties and McDonald's for the Backstreet Boys when they are on the move. Sometimes life on the road can get lonely or become a bit of a downer. To cure the blues, Nick's trick is to put on some headphones and just chill to some of his favorite music, like Metallica or Journey, or sit on his bunk bed and draw cartoons of the other guys. Brian also favors vegging out to some CDs and perhaps watching the world pass by through the bus windows. They are, after all, traveling in many very beautiful places, so there are usually a lot of interesting things to see.

One little trick the Boys used to have so the bus didn't take off without one of them: They had a little troll doll that they kept in the front of the bus, and whenever any of them stepped off the bus, he would leave the doll on the driver's seat so the driver would know that he didn't have all of his passengers. Pretty cool, huh?

Even after spending so much time together, the Boys never really fight about anything. If they have any disagreements, they are usually about minor stuff—almost like sibling quibbles. They might bicker a little about the CD player and about putting the CDs back in their cases so they don't get all gross. Also, Howie often hogs the bathroom, which is especially troublesome on long bus trips. Other than those minor tiffs, their life together is pretty harmonious in more ways than one!

Chowing Down on the Road

The Boys loved traveling through Europe, especially because it gave them a chance to see all the famous places and things that they had learned about in history and geography classes. Some of the guys were excited to try the foods of the different countries they were visiting, while the others were happy scanning the horizon for the golden arches of Mickey D's so they could chow down on some fries and burgers.

Howie is usually the leader of the adventurous eaters. In every country he visits, he likes to try something new. In the United Kingdom he sampled some fish and chips and also some Indian food, since a lot of people of Indian heritage live there and have opened authentic Indian restaurants.

Kevin also likes to taste different foods, but he admitted that when he is in Europe for long stretches of time, he gets homesick for American food and his mom's cooking, especially her chili.

The other three, A.J., Nick, and Brian, usually keep to what they know. Brian considers himself to be a meat-and-potatoes kind of guy, so he plays it safe with McDonald's and Kentucky Fried Chicken. A.J. is a little more bold when it comes to sampling other cuisines, but he admitted that they were frequent visitors to McDonald's in the U.K. because he thought the food there was just not good. In Germany, Switzerland, and Sweden they found some better stuff to chow down on, so they were a little more adventurous there.

Your Exclusive BSB Backstage Pass

When thousands of fans are waiting and screaming for their favorite Boys to come out onto the stage to perform, what are they doing backstage? How do they get ready to give the fans their all? Do they get nervous before shows?

Singing for an hour or two requires a lot of energy and stamina. In order to prepare for the shows, the Boys spend a lot of time before concerts warming up their voices—usually thirty minutes. They sing with each other a cappella to get ready, and practice some before the show begins. Another important thing to do is keep the vocal cords moist—that may sound strange, but it is actually an important part of the process, especially for Howie. He drinks a lot of hot herbal tea with lemon and honey before he heads out onto the stage. Sometimes he even uses a vaporizer and breathes in the warm, moist air.

On the flip side, Nick is not a tea drinker, so he doesn't follow Howie's teatime ritual. He basically spends his preshow time warming up his voice by singing scales or bits of songs.

The Boys are always on the move—if they are not actually performing, they are usually on their way to doing so. All that stress takes a toll on their bodies, including their voices. Sometimes taking a time-out or a mental break is the best thing they can do to chill out before they hit the stage. Sometimes Brian worries that his vocal cords are going to go into shock from belting out songs night after night, so he tries to take breaks whenever he can.

Kevin's trick is to stay away from dairy products before a show. Why? Not because he is lactose-intolerant, but because he says dairy foods produce a lot of mucus in the throat, which makes it hard to sing. That may seem gross, but if keeping away from milk and cheese works for him, then it's a smart move on Kevin's part.

A.J. is an all-around healthy person but is extra careful about maintaining his good health before performances. For instance, he is cautious about kissing fans at shows because he wants to avoid catching colds, which could bench him for a show or two or, worse, damage his voice. Getting the occasional cold is an inevitable prospect, especially when they're traveling all the time, so the minute he senses he might be getting sick, he gets on the phone to his doctor for a prescription and drinks some TheraFlu. This BSBer takes no chances when it comes to his health!

Right before the Boys hit the stage, they join hands, form a circle, and say a prayer together. Brian explains that this BSB ritual serves as a "focusing point" that helps them mentally prepare for what they want to accomplish during their performances. They also pray not only for their own safety, but also the safety of their fans.

However, it's not all serious business backstage before a show—the Boys have been known to pull a few practical jokes on one another! But sometimes it's not only the Boys who are the pranksters. Typically, the first and last nights of a tour are ripe for practical jokes—and the group's road crew are the ones who are trying to goof up the Boys! Howie recalls that the last show from one of their Christmas tours got really nutty. The Boys went out onstage to perform "Boys Will Be Boys," during which they were supposed to dance with their microphone stands. But instead of finding their microphones attached, there were carrots where the mikes should have been! After that, it was very hard to sing the song because the Boys couldn't stop laughing. The crew definitely got a kick out of that one.

Sometimes the Boys have a bit of downtime backstage. Each guy spends his little bit of extra time differently. Now that the Boys are big stars, they usually have hairdressers and makeup artists traveling with them. So Nick usually takes advantage of his preshow time and the availability of the hairdresser to keep his hair trimmed and neat.

A.J. spends his backstage time in a couple of ways. Sometimes he can be found winding up his other group members or the other artists with whom BSB is performing, playing pranks, or joking around. But other times he likes to mellow out by putting on his headphones and chilling to his favorite tunes, such as music by Brian McKnight. It helps him get away from it all before they go out onstage, especially since the Boys are so often surrounded by zillions of people.

Brian can usually be found joking around backstage. One of his favorite things to do—besides singing and dancing, of course—is making people laugh. He is generally in a happy, upbeat mood, and likes others to be in good moods along with him.

Apparently he does awesome Jim Carrey impressions, too!

Accidents Will Happen. . . .

Even though the Boys get a lot of practice doing their moves before they set out on a tour and especially by performing the same moves night after night, things don't always go smoothly during a concert. Usually these mishaps are unintended minor accidents and not because someone made a real mistake.

Once while singing the song "Get Down" during a concert in Germany, Howie really "got down"—or rather, he got knocked down! Apparently, while A.J. was doing his rap part of the song, Nick was on a small catwalklike part of the stage, doing his moves. Nick threw his arms out to the side and unintentionally knocked Howie off the stage—oops! Howie wasn't hurt badly, but it was kind of funny.

A little more seriously, Howie once slipped while he was onstage and then rolled to the edge! He was very fortunate that a nearby security guard was alert, grabbed hold of Howie's T-shirt, and held him so he wouldn't fall off the stage, which was very high. Another time A.J.'s shirt accidentally got caught in the percussionist's cymbals—and then he knocked over the entire percussion section. Surely that wasn't the sound the percussionist, Obie, was going for.

Sometimes things happen that are a bit more serious

than common mishaps, like one of the members getting sick or slightly injured while performing or touring. In 1995, while with the Boys on their first tour in Britain, Kevin got appendicitis and had to undergo an emergency operation to have his appendix removed. While Kevin was recovering from his surgery, the Boys had to go on performing as a foursome for some shows until he got better.

In March 1997 A.J. was caught in a mob of fans in Montreal and sprained his ankle as a result. He still managed to go onstage and perform for their concert later that night. A fun fact is that once he got his cast off, he let a Montreal radio station auction it off.

During the summer of 1997, there were rumors that Nick had fainted onstage during rehearsals for their American tour. When asked about it later, he clarified the story, explaining that he didn't actually faint. It was more that it was very hot and stuffy in the hall in which they were practicing and he felt woozy from the heat. He did go to the doctor, who said he should rest, so luckily nothing more serious happened.

Hang Time

When the Backstreet Boys are on tour, they usually don't have a heck of a lot of free time. But when they are able to snag some time for themselves, they try to do some shopping or hit a movie theater to catch some flicks. They also try to get in a game of hoops or shoot some pool, which they have gotten very good at.

What about those nights on tour when they are not

doing a show? Since they are not all of legal drinking age, they can't always go out together. On his nights off, Kevin likes to go out to a club, go dancing, or go for a drink. On Nick's free nights, he usually stays in his hotel room, playing Nintendo or watching TV.

If the Boys are in an exciting foreign country and they have some free time, they try to do as much sightseeing as they can. Once while the Boys were "down under" in Australia, they had enough free time to make an excursion to a wildlife park to meet some native inhabitants of that region—other than their Aussie fans, of course! On this little field trip were the five Boys; A.J.'s mom, Denise; Nick's mom, Jane; Brooke Harry, the publicist from Mushroom Records; and two very large bodyguards (in case the koalas got out of control).

The Boys saw a real Tasmanian devil, koalas, kangaroos (including baby joeys in their mothers' pouches), emus, an enormous wombat, some very noisy cockatoos, and a dingo. The Boys would have liked to stay longer, but then a mob of fans showed up clamoring for autographs, which the boys were happy to give them. All in all, the Boys were very pleased with their first sightseeing adventure in Aussie-land and meeting some of their fans, both human and animal.

Sometimes being away from home for so long makes them feel a bit homesick. To remind them of home, comfort them, or relieve some of the rigors of traveling, some of the guys try to have a ritual or carry a special object. Nick, not surprisingly, brings his Sega Playstation along, so he can get in a game of

Mortal Kombat or football whenever he gets the chance. Brian always eats peanut butter and jelly—he makes sure to carry a small supply in his bag wherever he goes. Howie likes to sleep in his Chinese silk PJ's—he always brings them with him on the road. A.J. used to be like Linus from the comic strip *Peanuts*, carrying around a blanket that his great-grandmother had knitted for him (see Chapter 6 for more on A.J. and his "blankey"). So what does Linus—er, A.J.—sleep with now that he no longer has his beloved blankey? His jeans, he says with a laugh—but perhaps he is only half joking.

The Boys all miss their families and homes when they are away. Luckily for Nick and A.J., Nick's father and A.J.'s mother have often traveled with them, so at least two of the Boys have a family member with them some of the time. The Boys especially miss the Sunshine State when they are traveling in the winter, since many places have very cold winter seasons. They love the beach and try to make a stop in sunny Florida whenever they can, even if it's just for a brief visit.

Celebrity Status

Because BSB has traveled so much and to so many different places, not only do they get to come up close to their fans, but they also get to connect with people *they* admire—celebrities in music, in particular. Whether they are sharing the spotlight, sharing a dressing room, or sharing some wisdom, the Boys have had more than simple star sightings!

Probably one of the first celebs that they met was Denniz PoP, of Ace of Base fame, who worked with BSB at the very beginning of their music career. Denniz produced the group's first single, "We've Got It Goin' On," in 1995 in Stockholm, Sweden, where his Cheiron Studios are located. So Denniz was instrumental (pun intended!) in helping the Boys launch themselves into the spotlight.

Throughout their travels, the Boys have gotten the op to meet the members of Color Me Badd and Boyz II Men as well as Whitney Houston and Bobby Brown! They also met Robbie Williams of Take That, who presented them with their first *Select* Award and gave them his words of wisdom about the importance of always remembering who they are and being appreciative of what they have. Good advice for everyone!

They have also met the Outhere Brothers (whose hit song was "Boom Boom Boom"), with whom Kevin got to do some secret partying. Once after doing some work with one of their producers in a studio, they came out to see Bryan Adams, the famous Canadian rocker! Since Kevin was a big fan, he asked for and got Bryan's autograph.

With which other famous artists did the Boys get to work on their music? For the single "Get Down (You're The One For Me)," the Boys got the chance to collaborate with Smooth T. from Fun Factory. P.M. Dawn produced BSB's version of the song "Set Adrift On Memory Bliss," since they were the ones who originally made that song famous in 1991. P.M. Dawn also worked with BSB on "If You Stay," which was included on the sound track for the movie *Booty Call*.

Babyface, who has penned hits for the likes of Whitney Houston and Eric Clapton, also wrote a tune for BSB, but unfortunately, he didn't have the time to produce the song. The Boys tried bringing in someone else, but they didn't love the end result. So the Boys have put their Babyface gem on the back burner until he himself has the time to work on it with them.

Once the Boys got the opportunity to sing for one of the music groups they most idolize: the Temptations! Since the Temptations have survived a very long time in the music business and have learned many things along the way, they wanted to help the Boys with their careers. One of the members of the Temptations advised the guys to be especially careful and pay attention to the business aspect of what they are doing. Being in a world-famous music group is as much about the business/financial part as it is about entertaining fans around the world and getting to do what they love best. The Boys took this advice to heart and soon thereafter set up their own corporation, called The Backstreet Boys, Inc. Doing this allowed them to jointly own shares in their company and make all business and financial decisions together.

Who are their favorites of the celebs they've met? Howie counts Jon Secada and Bow-Legged Lou from Full Force as his faves. Kevin names Boyz II Men and Sting. A.J. has three picks: Maxwell, No Mercy, and Chicago. Brian and Nick agree on their top celeb: Arnold Schwarzenegger.

They are buds with Boyzone, especially because they run into them often on the performance and promotion circuit. BSB often goes to check out Boyzone's shows and vice versa to show their support for one another.

When they were in Los Angeles in 1997 to shoot a video, their hotel was filled with tons of music stars who were also filming their videos. They got to meet the Quad City DJs, Dru Hill, Joe Blackstreet, Salt 'n' Pepa, and LL Cool J! "It must have been 'shoot your video in LA week,' " joked A.J.

Since they are now traveling in the same circles, the Boys have also met the Spice Girls several times! What do the Boys think of the Girls, their British megastar counterparts? They think the Girls are "really cool," especially because they are friendly to them and always ask how things are going. Actually, they once shared a dressing room with them at a show they did in Germany. The camera crews kept coming in and out to film these two superhot groups together. Unfortunately, everyone was already dressed for the show by the time the press got there, so only the ten of them know what happened behind that closed door. And the Boys and the Girls once took some time out to pose for a great snapshot. They all looked really happy—it was clear from their faces that they are all enjoying their lives and their success. They also looked like they could either go out on a really wild quintuple date—or at least burn up the stage if they ever performed together!

CHAPTER 11

Doin' It BSB Style

When it comes to phat, funky, slammin' style, the Backstreet Boys definitely have got it goin' on! Even though these handsome hunks would look good wearing garbage bags, these Boys know how to dress for success. From clothes to accessories, from hairstyles to sneakers, they wear it all well! Even their individual tastes in music and food are cool. While you won't see them looking the same for too long, you will see them looking good all the time. "The truth is," Howie says, "that we like changing our image, trying everything new." Which means that in the three years that they have been on the music scene, their look has gone from youthful and boyish to sophisticated and sexy.

Cool Clothes

Since the Boys are a group and have to make public appearances together constantly, a unified yet funky image is important. At the same time, the Boys don't allow their stylists complete control over their group look. It is important to the Boys to be on the cutting edge of the fashion front, so they make suggestions to their stylists about what look is in or what style they like. On the flip side, they don't want to look too done up or overly trendy, because they want their fans to be able to relate to them. So when the Boys are putting together their BSB image, they always try to come up with the perfect balance with the help of their stylists.

The Boys don't always dress exactly alike, but usually their look is coordinated in one way or the other so that their outfits complement one another. For instance, they all might be wearing the same style shirt, but the colors might be different. Or they might all be wearing the same kind of shirt, say a hockey shirt, but the colors or logos on them won't be the same. Sometimes their outfits are different for the most part, but they will each wear one piece or the same color that ties all of their looks together.

On the cover of their U.S. CD, for instance, the Boys are dressed in black jeans, black T-shirts, and black Doc Marten–type shoes, but each one appears to be wearing a different kind of boxy jacket—four of them are wearing tan jackets, and Kevin is wearing a dark brown jacket. The result is that they have a sleek, unified look, but don't appear to be quintuplets.

The Boys have worn everything from slick black suits to football jerseys. Some of the sports gear they have worn publicly includes: hockey shirts, gear from the 1996 Summer Olympics in Atlanta, snowboarding outfits, basketball tanks over T-shirts, and ski jackets. What about brand-name clothes or clothes with logos?

Those include Tommy Hilfiger, Fila, Nike, Adidas, and Timberland. As a group, their look sometimes is very hip-hop and urban in style: lots of baggy pants, oversized shirts, brightly colored windbreakers, and sneakers.

As the Boys get a little older, a more recent trend seems to be that they are moving toward a kind of funky prepster look: lots of jeans, both black and blue; button-down shirts open to reveal T-shirts underneath; maybe different kinds of jackets or blazers. This look is somewhat more sophisticated and works well on them as they leave their teen years behind.

Between the Boys' music videos, their concerts, and their public appearances, the Boys' image has been everywhere: in magazines, in newspapers, on television, on the Web. But would the Boys choose the same clothes they wear for their official moments as members of the Backstreet Boys for times when they are just hanging out, not working? Not necessarily.

For instance, for photo shoots, many times the Boys don't get to choose what they wear—the photographers or magazine stylists choose. And what they pick isn't necessarily what the Boys would consider their style. Once they did a photo shoot for a magazine in Europe, which made the Boys wear these corny Halloween-type costumes. But the Boys saw the humor in the situation. Brian chose a Batman outfit, but his ears were totally sticking out, so the Boys nicknamed him "Rat Boy." Sometimes they have a completely opposite problem, like when they did a shoot in Canada. The problem wasn't that the stylist wanted the Boys to wear cheesy clothes, but that they wanted them to wear practically *no* clothes. They were asked to pose in underwearlike shorts and T-shirts, which was a weird experience for the guys.

In a recent issue of *BB* magazine, the Boys were interviewed about their fashion sense. The mag also did a photo shoot of the guys but, knowing they are sensitive about what they wear (and not wanting to make the same mistake as that European mag that dressed the Boys up in silly costumes), the *BB* people let them choose their look. The guys wore their own jeans, sneakers, and accessories such as watches (silver for Kev, a black sports watch for Howie), silver bracelets (Howie, A.J., and Kevin), silver rings (Kevin and Howie), and of course A.J. had on some funky silver-rimmed shades. Then each wore different-colored Gap polo shirts: Kevin and Brian wore sky blue, Nick wore turquoise, A.J.'s was royal blue, and Howie's was lime green. They looked great in them, too! After the shoot, the Boys autographed their shirts so *BB* could offer their readers the chance to win the very shirts worn by the Boys! There are now five lucky winners out there who own one of these special shirts.

Personal Style

These are five guys who *love* to shop for clothes. Wherever they are, they take any chance they get to hit the stores and snag some new duds. Each of them has his own personal style, which reflects his individual taste and personality.

Howie D. Style: Howie D. prefers to go against whatever is *au courant* at the moment. He likes to be different, so if tight pants are in, then Howie D. will wear baggy pants, and vice versa. In general, Howie prefers to buy somewhat tight-fitting clothes for his nights out clubbing. He might choose a retro kind of shirt and close-fitting jeans rather than the big, baggy look that the BSB often have to wear. Howie was into Tommy Hilfiger clothes for a while but seems to have moved on to different designers. His favorite items of clothing are his many vests, of all different kinds.

A.J. Style: A.J.'s taste in clothes goes the opposite way from Howie's—he likes his clothes *big,* the baggier the better. He is actually a size 30 in pants, but he always buys clothes several sizes too big on purpose. He'll buy T-shirts that are XXL or pants that are a size 36! At one point A.J. was trying out hip-hop clothes by a fresh new label called Dada, which is owned by a really young guy who is only around twenty years old. Other designers he digs: Tommy Hilfiger, Calvin Klein, and DKNY.

Kevin Style: Since Kevin is the oldest, his personal style in clothes tends to come down more on the mature side of things. When he dresses up for nicer, more formal events, he likes to wear a linen blazer and a button-down shirt. He also looks hot in black leather jackets. That is not to say Kevin doesn't own some football shirts and jeans; he likes to dress down just as much as any of the other guys.

B-Rok Style: Brian has always had a thing for tattoos. He is also into wearing some jewelry. In some of the BSB music videos Brian is sporting studs in both ears. When not shooting videos, he sometimes wears them and sometimes doesn't. He also has worn different chains around his neck. For instance, in the "Get Down" vid he wears a silver chain with a big cross. When he was in Australia he got a gold chain with a "B-Rok" pendant, which he says he loves a lot.

Nick Style: Nick usually decides what to wear by the way he is feeling. Sometimes he prefers comfortable clothes such as sportswear and big jerseys. But if he feels like wearing something more alternative, he will. Or if he's in a preppy mood, then he'll go for a preppy look.

Some of the guys even swap or borrow each other's clothes. Sometimes there is a little petty thievery going on—A.J. might actually borrow his friends' clothes and sometimes not give them back! If you opened up A.J.'s closet, a lot of the clothes there might not be his! Howie usually stays out of such exchanges because he tends to be more particular about his stuff—and because he doesn't want to risk never seeing a favorite shirt or jacket again. He's no dummy.

Awesome Accessories

Each guy also seems to add his own personal style to whatever he's wearing, whether it is A.J.'s sunglasses, Kevin's earrings, Brian's sideways baseball cap, Howie's silver bracelets, or Nick's boyish grin. As a group, accessories play a big part. At any given time—whether they're working or not—invariably you'll see a Backstreet Boy wearing silver chain bracelets and necklaces, studs or hoops (or sometimes both at the same time), silver rings, leather bracelets, a chunky silver watch, a baseball cap, or of course sunglasses.

Happening Hair

One of the fun advantages of being in the public eye all the time and being in a business in which looks are very important is morphing your image into something new whenever you want. You can experiment with the latest trends and try out the newest looks. The Boys are no exception to this rule, especially when it comes to hairstyles. Throughout their five-year career, each Boy has been through several different hair colors and cuts—some of them good, some of them . . . well, not so good.

Nick's straight blond hair has gone from long on the sides with a middle part, giving way to darker roots, to no part with the bangs brushed down the front of his forehead, to slicked up and back in the front, so that some of his hair falls to the side, while the rest is slicked back. Lately Nick has been wearing his hair shorter than he had in the past. Why's that? A few reasons. First, he was just plain sick of his hair parted down the middle. He wanted to update his image and try to be a bit more sophisticated-looking. Also, Nick was having problems with fans and his longer hair. It wasn't that his fans didn't groove on his long hair—it was that sometimes fans would grab on to it when BSB was moving through crowds of people! It was almost dangerous for him to have his hair long enough to hold on to—he was actually fearful that one day someone would yank a bunch of it out of his head. Also, it's easy for him to keep his hair short while he's on tour, because the group often has a hair stylist with them. That makes trims an easy and painless experience!

Howie's dark brown hair has been through a lot of changes. His hair is very curly and can be difficult to control. He has had his hair all different lengths—from almost shoulder-length, with curls free and wild, to shorn very close to his scalp, and everything in between. For a while his hair was on the very short side, though not so closely shaven. When he lets it grow a little longer, he slicks it back with what looks like some mighty strong gel and perhaps grows out his sideburns. Sometimes he pulls his hair back in a tight ponytail, which gives him a sleeker look.

Brian's hairstyle has stayed somewhat consistent throughout his career. Usually he wears his hair short around the sides and back, with the front a little longer and either brushed straight forward in a Caesar cut or a bit longer in front, which tends to get a little wavy. He has played around with his hair color, going between dirty blond and reddish brown. He tends to experiment more with his facial hair—maybe longer sideburns or a goatee. Brian's strong square jaw allows him to carry off these looks well.

A.J. tends to keep his thick dark brown hair very short. When it is a little longer on top, he likes to gel it, giving it the "wet look." Instead of length, A.J. experiments more with hair color. He went platinum blond for a little while. When A.J.'s mother saw his new blond 'do, she almost flipped. She eventually got used to it, but for a while she would look at his platinum blond hair, shake her head, and say, "Oh, my God!" Since he relies on his ever-changing array of sunglasses as his accessory of choice, A.J. often opts for different styles of facial hair, such as a thin mustache, long sideburns, or a goatee.

Kevin's hairstyles have progressively gotten more confident. For a time he wore his black hair longish around the sides and very long in the front, practically hiding his thick, strong eyebrows, in a sort of mop-top style. He sometimes would slick it to the sides in order to keep his long bangs out of his handsome face. Recently his hair has become much shorter, with short bangs brushed down on his forehead—not nearly as long and thick as in earlier days. Sometimes he gels it to make the top spiky. Kevin, too, has been known to sport a goatee and mustache, setting off his thick eyebrows and his deep blue-green eyes.

Much Music!

When it comes to musical tastes, the Boys veer off in all sorts of directions. Their eclectic musical style as a group is reflected in their personal music picks.

A.J.: A.J. likes rap, R&B, and hip-hop music. He listens to Dru Hill, Jamiroquai, Maxwell, Mark Morrisson, Boyz II Men, Az Yet, Brian McKnight, Babyface, and Rick James.

Howie: Howie usually names Jon Secada as his most major musical influence. He also grooves on the Artist Formerly Known As Prince, Celine Dion, New Edition, Bobby Brown, Michael Jackson, Al B. Sure, Phillip Bailey and Earth, Wind & Fire, and other soul and R&B music.

Brian: Brian loves a variety of artists, including Boyz II Men, Madonna, Mariah Carey, Bobby Brown, Janet Jackson, Luther Vandross, Take Six, Brian McKnight, Babyface, and, of course, the Backstreet Boys!

Nick: Nick loves Steve Perry and Journey, even though he was quite young when they were popular. In fact, during concerts, Nick sometimes sings his favorite Journey songs, such as "Open Arms." He also digs Nirvana, Jodeci, Oasis, Shai, Michael Jackson, and Notorious B.I.G.

Kevin: Like Kevin's taste in food, his taste in music encompasses everything from classical to soul. For instance, Kevin considers some of the tracks on *Life After Death* by Notorious B.I.G. "really phat" (though he cautions that it is not a "family-oriented" album). He also listens to older pop, Maxwell, Boyz II Men, R. Kelly, Babyface, Michael Jackson, Teddy Riley, and Brian McKnight, as well as country artist Clint Black.

Celluloid Style

When it comes to looking good on film, the Backstreet Boys can't be beat. Even though they used the same director (Lionel C. Martin) for their first four videos, their style has certainly changed—and matured. They have come a long way from spraying each other with water hoses while washing a Jeep (as they did in their first video, for "We've Got It Goin' On") and frolicking on the ski slopes with girls, snowmen, and sleds (as they did in the video for "I'll Never Break Your Heart").

The video for the hit song "Quit Playing Games (With My Heart)," which was directed by Kai Sehr, was shot in a schoolyard in Orlando (not far from their homes) and is their most heart-wrenching. By the time the rain comes pouring down, drenching the pleading, heartbroken Boys, it is hard to imagine anyone even attempting not to play it straight with these romantic, sensitive guys.

One of their most recent videos is also one of their

slickest looks-wise. The video for "As Long As You Love Me," their second hit single in the U.S., was filmed in downtown Pasadena, California, in the Royal Laundry warehouse building. The video was directed by Nigel Dick, from Britain, and their choreographer was Fatima, who has also created moves for Brandy and Whitney Houston. However, not all of BSB's moves in the vid are choreographed. A bit of what they do is just the Boys being, well, the Boys. A stylist with whom they have worked on other things helped them pick out the coordinating but different tan and brown outfits that they wear in the video.

Some U.S. fan magazines were on hand to watch the filming of the video and interview the Boys between takes. The Boys said they had a great time making the video for "As Long As You Love Me." They thought the girls who appeared in the video were really nice. At times, Nick admitted, it was hard to work because their female costars were so pretty and fun to be around. By the looks of it, they must have managed to get their work done, considering how the video went to the top of the charts!

As the Boys continue to grow both artistically and in years, you can bet that their tastes, looks, and all-around style will grow with them. It will be exciting to see what happens next!

CHAPTER 12

Keeping the Backstreet Pride Alive!

In the liner notes of the Backstreet Boys' U.S. CD, Howie gives a long, heartfelt thank-you to BSB's fans all over the world. He stresses the fact that the band couldn't have gotten where they are today without their devoted fans.

His words are sincere—not to mention true.

Every success, every achievement, and every award the Backstreet Boys have is mostly because of two things: their hard work and the devotion of their fans! Without the continuing support of their fans all over the world, the Backstreet Boys couldn't have made it to the top. And they know it, which is why they are always thanking them. It has always been a two-way street for these Boys—they never take without giving something in return. That's one of the things that make them so special—and why the fans love them so much.

And the fans sure do show their love in lots of different and sometimes kooky ways. When it comes to keeping the Backstreet pride alive, these fans know how to raise the roof!

The Boys and Their Fans

Ultimately, the fans are what make it possible for the Boys to make their music and tour all over the world. "One of the most gratifying things is seeing people sing your songs out in the audience along with you," Howie once said. In the end, the Boys do what they do *for* the fans, so they are appreciative of the devotion and attention they get from people everywhere they go.

The Boys even know a lot of their fans by name, especially those who often follow the Boys while they are on tour. The guys like to be in close contact with the girls and allow them to take their pictures, or they sign autographs for them. Once they met some fans and invited them to meet for breakfast, said A.J. If they have asked for the phone numbers of certain fans they have met, the Boys will try to call them to rap and get to know them a little better. A.J. had become friendly with a fan in Germany, so he once called with a special phone card the Boys all have. She was really surprised to hear from a Backstreet Boy! He and the fan talked about all kinds of things, like interests, school, and hobbies, and then he asked her to come to their concert the next time their tour brought BSB through her city.

Since the British fans were among the first fans of the Backstreet Boys, the guys have gotten to know some of their more dedicated fans pretty well. Whenever they return to that country, the guys will actually sit on the plane wondering if so-and-so will be meeting them at the airport or if another regular will turn up for a visit at their hotel. The Boys look forward to seeing some of these fans time and again, because many of them have become their friends.

In the early days of BSB, the Boys could hang out in the lobby of their hotels and stay up late chatting with their fan friends who would come visit them. But it has become more and more difficult to do that, as more fans have started showing up at the Boys' hotel. Sometimes the group becomes quite large and causes a major headache for the hotel people, so lately security has become tighter in the hotels in which the Boys stay when they tour. If things do get a little raucous, the hotel security people ask the fans to leave and send the Boys back up to their rooms, which can be a bummer for everyone.

The Boys get hundreds of fan letters each week. When the Boys first started out, each member tried to answer all of his fan mail personally, but when the group became popular in so many places and started to receive tons of mail, it became much tougher to answer them all. They do try to write personal greetings whenever they can.

When the guys go toward the edge of the stage during a concert—on purpose—they can sometimes hear what the girls in the first row are saying to them. So, what do these first-row girls say? Some of their comments can't be repeated here, but they usually tell the Boys how much they love them and their music and ask the Boys if they will dedicate a song to them.

Many girls actually cry at their concerts, especially

when the Boys are singing their most romantic love songs. When the BSBers take off their tops and show off their hunky bods in concert, the girls just go wild! Some lucky fans get asked to go up onstage and dance with one of the Boys. And sometimes one of the guys will give them a rose, showing off their romantic side.

What kind of presents from fans do the Boys like the most? Nick loves jewelry, so he is happy to receive gold jewelry from girls. Howie agrees about the jewelry, but he also likes teddy bears. Once a girl gave Brian a small basketball hoop that he could bring with him wherever he went, to hang up and shoot hoops whenever he wanted to. He thought that was a sweet gift.

Brian admits that he feels badly that he and the guys don't get to spend as much time as they used to with their original fans because there are always new people who want to meet and talk to them. Many fans in the United Kingdom (one of the first places where they became popular) feel that the Boys don't spend enough time there, but as Brian explains it, the Boys have to spread out their visits among several other countries now, especially the United States, because, he says, "We're trying to conquer the whole world."

So for those of you who feel that you don't get enough BSB in person wherever you live, Brian says, "What I want everyone to realize is that the fans always have been, and always will be the most important thing. After all, we'd be nothing without them."

Fans in the Audience

Fans who are in the first few rows often throw presents for the Boys onto the stage while they are performing. They throw all kinds of stuff that they think the Boys will like. Once a fan threw a stuffed bear onto the stage and accidentally hit A.J. on the head with it. Not to worry—he didn't get seriously injured or anything, but his head did hurt for a couple of days.

Fans also sometimes throw their underwear, which Nick thinks is kind of funny, since it is totally weird to be singing surrounded by a bunch of bras. Kevin added that once when he was playing the piano a bra fell on his face. Brian said that when they were doing a concert in Manchester, England, a fan threw a red bra up onstage, so Bri picked it up and threw it at one of the security guards. One particularly bold girl, A.J. recalls, took off her T-shirt and bra and then called out his name. Once he saw her, he was so shocked that he forgot to continue with the song he was singing. Nick saw this whole thing happening and, he said, "got paralyzed," too. At first he didn't think she would go all the way and take off her undergarment, but then she did, so he was totally surprised.

Sometimes fans in the audience can get too aggressive. They try to grab the Boys' hands and legs in an effort to get closer to them. Howie said that he has fallen off the stage at least a couple of times because of fans who were trying to touch him.

After the shows, many female fans follow the Boys back to their hotel. Some very brazen, resourceful girls get through to them on the phone by telling the hotel receptionists that they are relatives. Sometimes they manage to get up to their actual hotel room doors and knock! If the fans are lucky, the Boys will open the door, talk to them a bit, maybe pose for some pictures with them, and sign some autographs. Nick said that he wouldn't mind getting some copies of that kind of snapshot so he could put them in a photo album commemorating their various tours. Ultimately they send the girls away so they can get some sleep, since they are usually so wiped after a grueling concert.

The Boys do like to talk and communicate with their fans on a regular basis. In fact, they usually spend some time with some of their most loyal fans before each show. A.J. said that he likes to hear what their audience thinks of their music and what they are doing. Nick is into meeting the girls so he can become friends with some of them. He thinks it is cool to have friends from all over the world and learn about different cultures. He often takes their numbers and addresses so he can keep in touch with them and maybe see them when he returns to their cities or countries.

Since touring doesn't allow time to form lasting intimate relationships, the Boys usually maintain the just-friends status with the girls they meet. Since they travel all the time and are never in one place for very long, it just doesn't seem fair to them to become emotionally connected, only to have to leave again so soon. Even if they see or meet someone they think is special, there is not much they can do to pursue a relationship, because before they know it, they are on the road to someplace new.

Guys in the House, Too

The Backstreet Boys also have guy fans, which pleases them. In a way, it feels like a bigger accomplishment if the Boys' music reaches guys as well as girls, since it is like peer approval. When a guy compliments the band, it is a sign of respect that all the Boys appreciate. Sometimes, however, guys in the audience might be obnoxious out of jealousy, perhaps because they see the Boys doing something they want to be doing and getting tons of attention, or because they see their girlfriends and female friends swooning for BSB. Some teenage male fans have thrown things at the Boys in the streets, which is just totally uncool with the Boys.

Foreign Fans' Face-Off

Both A.J. and Nick think that the group's European fans are more aggressive in general than fans from other areas. While in London one time early on in BSB history, A.J. and Howie decided to walk around Piccadilly Circus, a very bustling, touristy, commercial area that boasts tons of shopping, theaters, and restaurants. The two were looking for a place to eat (lots of American fast-food restaurants there!) and waiting for some friends to join them. Suddenly some fans recognized the two guys and came up to them. Before they knew it, they were surrounded by fans from all over Europe who were visiting London. A.J. and Howie didn't want to disappoint their fans and they didn't have any security people with them to fend off the attention, so the guys stood there and signed autographs for more than an hour. They did eventually meet up with their friends and find a place to chow down for dinner—they must have been famished by then!

The German fans are perhaps the most avid of the European fans. A.J. said that in Germany fans would follow the Boys around in taxis or even stay at the same hotels where the Boys would stay when they were touring. Girls would give them presents. Some girls would go to every single show in that area and act all wild at the show. Some even fainted when the Boys would come out onstage. But probably the most fervent of the German fans were two girls who climbed over a barbed-wire fence, ripping their clothes, and sneaked into the Boys' hotel room. The Boys were surprised not only to see these girls in their room, but also when they found out how they got there in the first place!

Fans sometimes can get out of control. It is understandable in a way, especially when some fans wait for hours, sometimes even overnight, just to catch sight of the guys. It's not that they are trying to cause any harm or purposely cause disturbances, but sometimes their excitement reaches a fevered pitch and chaos ensues.

When the Boys appeared for the second time on VIVA, the German MTV-type channel, during their first European tour, there was a major not-so-good fan incident outside of the studio. What happened was that VIVA was so excited about having BSB back for a second time, they publicized the appearance for the whole week before the show. So by the day of the appearance, two hundred girls were waiting outside for the Boys to show up at the studio. In order to get a glimpse of the Boys, the fans started climbing and jumping over the parked cars, and the soft-topped convertibles ended up getting holes punched through their roofs. Even though the incident wasn't the Boys' fault, VIVA told BSB they couldn't come back again. However, the channel didn't hold to their threat, since the popularity of the Backstreet Boys in Germany is just too big to ignore. In fact, on March 28, 1998, the Boys went back to VIVA to do an *Unplugged* show for the channel!

There have been incidents, too, at record-store signings and other appearances. Sometimes the Boys get a bigger fan turnout than they can handle. Once in Germany the Boys were at a store to sign CDs and there was practically a riot! They were able to sign only a handful of CDs before fans broke through the barricades. Unfortunately, these overzealous fans were destructive as well as eager. They trashed the store, tearing down posters and in-store displays. As a result, the Boys had to leave the place, because they were concerned for their own safety.

Kevin said that they have found the girls to be the shyest in Japan. In Japan, the Boys even go up to the girls—but they just blush and lower their heads because they are so shy.

But in contrast, the fans in Spain are passionate! The night before the Backstreet Boys were scheduled to make a free concert appearance at a department store called El Corte Inglés, in the center of Madrid, five hundred girls were camped out, prepared to sleep overnight in the hopes of catching a glimpse of their fave group the next day, or better yet, scoring an autograph. But by the morning of the event, a crowd of five hundred had been transformed into a horde of fifteen thousand eager fans!

Because this was no ordinary turnout, the city authorities became seriously worried about how to handle security. The store and city hall had agreed to provide security and medical services—but they hadn't counted on a crowd of fifteen thousand people! So they had no other choice than to cancel the event.

This set off a wave of upset and panic throughout the crowd of fans, many of whom had been waiting hours. Some took off in search of the hotel in which the Boys were staying, while others showed their displeasure outside the radio station that was broadcasting the event.

At 4:00 P.M. the Boys gave a press conference at their hotel, saying that they were upset that they were unable to appear and perform for their loyal fans. Kevin Richardson commented, "Our fans' security is our number one concern," and explained why they had to cancel the event at the last minute. They promised they would reschedule the event in November when they returned to Madrid and that they would be better prepared to handle such a large crowd. After the press conference, since the Boys couldn't mingle with the fans because of security issues, they waved to people from their hotel balcony.

The fans were only somewhat satisfied by this

explanation and took a long time to calm down. Some people stayed outside the Boys' hotel, which caused nightmarish traffic jams. The local authorities then had to become involved to clear out the crowd.

But wherever the Backstreet Boys go, it seems there are screaming or fainting fans. For example, when the Boys performed at a shopping mall in Montreal, thirty-five girls fainted. Still, despite different crazy happenings, the Boys love their fans. They know the fans just want to be near them, and that makes the guys feel good about what they are doing.

There's No Place Like Home . . . the BSB's Homes!

Even the Boys' private homes are not sacred. Fans from both the States and abroad have tracked down their houses and relatives. Some sort of fan disturbance is a frequent occurrence for the Littrell, Richardson, McLean, Carter, and Dorough families, both immediate and extended. Kevin's grandfather, for example, has had German fans pay him a visit looking for Kevin. The Boys' families try to be as courteous as possible to the fans, especially those who make an extra-special effort or who have traveled a long way. One girl from another country who was visiting family in Ohio drove down to Lexington, Kentucky, and made contact with Brian's family. Bri's mother told the girl that although she would have to draw the line at letting her visit the house, she would meet the girl for breakfast. The young girl gave a fan letter to Bri's mom to pass on to her son. So of course Bri's mother made sure that he took the time to write back!

Howie told *Smash Hits* magazine in England that some fans went to his house on Mother's Day to give his mom flowers and chocolates. She was so touched (and embarrassed) by this gesture that she actually invited them to come into the house for dinner!

Nick's home, however, seems to be the biggest target for all kinds of incidents. Fans used to go right up onto his family's lawn and into their garden. Apparently there was a guy in town who was selling maps with directions to get to Nick's house! This guy went so far as to hire a bus to bring thirty people a day by Nick's house. These people would pick the flowers right out of the Carters' garden to take home as souvenirs! Nick's family had to have a high fence erected around their home and property to discourage trespassers.

Some fans have even disturbed the Carter family on Christmas! The family was about to sit down to dinner when some fans showed up. Nick, always the gentleman, went outside to sign autographs for them. Then the fans showed up again the next day! But this time they came to apologize for disturbing the Carters' Christmas. Their explanation was that getting Nick to sign his autograph was their Christmas present to themselves.

One time Nick's house was in the audience! What does that mean? One girl had taken a picture of Nick's house, blown it up to poster size, written on it "I was there," and held it up while the Boys were performing onstage. Nick was bewildered and said to Brian,

"My house is in the audience!" And sure enough, there it was.

There are many stories about fans who actually find out the telephone numbers of the Boys' families and sometimes even speak to one of their family members. But what happens when they get the wrong number from the operator? Well, they might get Dahlia McLean or Gerald Richardson! Dahlia's phone number is listed under her husband's name, which happens to be Alexander James McLean—as in A.J.—and Kevin's late father's name was Jerald! These two people—who, by the way, are not relatives of the famous Boys—have been getting calls from enthusiastic fans for more than a year! Since many of these calls are from overseas, these two innocent bystanders often get these calls in the middle of the night. Gerald Richardson has gotten calls from as far away as Norway, Belgium, Spain, Slovenia, Puerto Rico, and Italy, and instead of changing his number or making it unlisted, he actually welcomes the chance to talk to people from all over the world. Now that is patience and open-mindedness!

Minor Mishaps

Sometimes minor mishaps are the result not of the fans themselves, but of the very things that are meant to protect the Boys from too many fans. Once when the Boys were making an appearance in Montreal, they were mobbed by an amazing number of fans— something like ten thousand people! But that isn't the noteworthy part of the story, since that was happening more and more. What is ironic is that when the van came to pick them up, it ran over A.J.'s foot! He wasn't hurt too badly, but he did have to go to the hospital and wasn't able to perform in two shows.

Another mishap happened in Holland, but this time to Howie. Since there were too many people outside their hotel, the Boys had to slip through a window to get into their van. On the Boys' way out, a girl grabbed Howie's backpack and yanked him down onto the ground. (Strong girl!) He still has the scars to prove it—which he shows on the video portion of the enhanced version of the U.S. CD.

Over the Top

Sometimes there's just no stopping the most ardent BSB supporters. Some fans will go to great lengths just to catch a glimpse. They'll hang around outside the airports from or to which they know the Boys will be flying, or they'll set up camp outside the places where the Boys are scheduled to make an appearance.

Some fans are so dedicated that they travel all over the world to see the Boys wherever they are. Once two female fans, one from Germany and one from Switzerland, were waiting for Brian when he got home to Orlando. Apparently a picture of his car was published in a magazine, so they stationed themselves near it to wait for him to get home. They came prepared with stuff to get his autograph and were so excited when he finally showed up!

Other fans have been known to be even more adventurous and daring than that. The Boys have had stowaways on their tour bus! Girls frequently sneak onto their tour bus while the luggage is being loaded into the bottom of the bus. Once they get inside, they'll hide out in the bathroom until the guys find them.

The *Daily News* in New York reported about two fans who stowed away on one of the BSB's tour buses—but not in the bathroom. These fans somehow got into the luggage compartment under the bus and weren't discovered there for the entire duration of the trip! When the bus finally arrived at its destination, the fans were suffering from dehydration. They are lucky that they didn't suffer bigger health hazards than that—and we can only hope that these devoted fans actually got the chance to meet the Boys after all that effort and risk!

What happens when these determined fans finally reach the object of their desires? Nick says one of two things usually happens: "Either they don't know what to do and they just stand there or they attack us, pretty much." Some fans must be so surprised that they actually made it face-to-face with their beloved Boys that they become paralyzed once they are in the BSB's presence.

While the guys *love* the attention and appreciate the dedication of their fans all over the world, they do sometimes worry about their fans' safety and well-being. Since some fans attempt somewhat wild stunts to get in the presence of the Boys, they could potentially hurt themselves. It is also sometimes scary for the Boys themselves, especially when a fan is really out of control and is pulling and grabbing at the Boys' clothes—or, as was noted before, Nick's hair. (That's why Nick now keeps his hair short!)

Some fans just want to get their hands on some object that the Boys have touched or, better yet, that belongs to the Boys. As a result, the Boys have had some of their personal stuff swiped by fans, such as sunglasses, hats, and jewelry. But there are times when fans don't even wait until someone's back is turned to take something—they will try to take something that the Boys are still wearing! A.J. has even had a hoop earring ripped right out of his ear when he leaned over to give a fan a kiss! Episodes like that ruin it for everyone, because they make the Boys more cautious and hesitant about getting close to their fans.

Virtual Backstreet Pride

In October 1997 the Backstreet Boys became super-virtual when their newly enhanced official Web site was launched. As noted earlier, fans all over the world had been waiting months, even years, for the site to go up, so by October the demand for it was huge. An official press release from the site said that in its first days the site received so many hits, it had to shut down *three* times over the first weekend, despite the state-of-the-art technology powering it.

Peter Bjorklund, president of Carlson Sterling Global Media, which is the official development and marketing company that created the site for the Backstreet

Boys and their record label, Jive Records, said, "These numbers are unheard of on a daily basis. . . . We can only count visitors who got through," which means that there were probably even more fans who were trying to get onto the site. Bjorklund went on to say that the BSB site has gotten as many hits in a day as some Web sites for music artists that already have a huge, established following in the United States get in a month or even a year.

But even back before the super-duper, newly enhanced Web site was launched, BSB's first official site, www.backstreetboys.com, was voted the fifth most searched Web site for any musical group or musical artist on the Internet, according to Lycos Websearch and *People* magazine. In June 1997, for example, the site was averaging thirty thousand hits per day.

The updated site also boasts a premium pay service called the "VIP Section" for which fans can pay a fee to get special exclusive info, pics, interviews, sneak previews, and interactive chats. This part went on-line in November 1997.

Fans around the world also show their own particular brand of Backstreet pride on-line. Not only do they participate in chats, post messages to each other on electronic bulletin boards, and send E-mails about BSB sightings, but they also create and host several of their own unofficial Web sites, virtual fan clubs, and Web rings. There are sites hosted by fans in Singapore, France, Brazil, Canada, England, Poland, Spain, and the United States, among many others. (Check out the Resource Guide at the end of the book for some

URL listings, site reviews, and tips for conducting
BSB Web searches.) Of course, these sites vary in
quality, comprehensiveness, and depth, but each site
has a distinct personality of its own and usually offers
some tidbits of information that can't be found on
another fan site. Many of them have photos, bios of
the members, group history, concert reviews, links to
other sites of interest, the latest news and gossip, chat
rooms, bulletin boards, surveys, and guest books.

The best part about these sites is that they allow
fans from all over the world to find out what fans in
other countries are saying, thinking, experiencing, and
feeling about the Backstreet Boys. Since the Web is a
fairly new medium and more and more kids are log-
ging on, having a worldwide virtual community of
fans is a relatively new phenomenon that was not possible even as recently as when the Backstreet Boys
first formed, five years ago. The proliferation of these
unofficial fan Web sites have made a major contribu-
tion toward the overall success of the Backstreet Boys.

How Do the Fans Rate the Boys?

Many of the unofficial BSB Web sites conduct
fan surveys to allow the fans to voice their personal
opinions, from their favorite songs to their favorite
member.

When it comes to choosing a favorite BSB
member, there seems to be heavy competition
between Nick and Brian, just as the two have between
them in real life! On one site, Nick was chosen as the

best dancer in BSB, with Brian and A.J. close behind. Results in categories such as favorite BSB song and favorite BSB video vary widely, since not all of the same singles have been released in every country. So the results depend more on what country the people who visit the site are from. One site asked fans where they would most like to go on a dream date with their favorite Backstreet Boy. The beach topped the list, with places like a museum, a park, an amusement park, the movies, and a play tying for second place.

I asked two dedicated fans from London, Sarah Cohen and Rachel Cohen—two sisters who were early supporters of the Backstreet Boys—to tell us what they love about BSB. Here's what they had to say:

I love the Backstreet Boys. My favorite Boy is Brian. I think he has the cutest face and I love the color of his hair. My favorite BSB song is "As Long As You Love Me." I love how they sing the song, especially because it shows how good their voices are. The video for "Everybody (Backstreet's Back)" is my favorite because it really keeps you on your feet. All of my friends also love the Backstreet Boys.

The English pop music magazines, such as *Smash Hits*, *Live and Kicking*, *Shout*, and *Top of the Pops*, have articles about the Backstreet Boys all the time. These magazines usually have interviews with the Boys, as well as BSB posters, photographs, song lyrics, concert dates, and stickers.

Nick is a favorite with many English BSB fans. Fans in England also like the fact that the Backstreet Boys are American because they add an international feeling in London. The Boys appeal to both boys and girls in England. The girls love BSB, think they are gorgeous, and like their music very much. The boys like BSB because they are good role models for them. Male fans also like BSB's music, too.

From a *big* Backstreet Boys fan,

Sarah Victoria Cohen
London, England

Hi, my name is Rachel. Brian is my favorite Backstreet Boy. "Everybody (Backstreet's Back)" is both my favorite BSB song and video. I like it because it is produced really well and the effects are wicked.

I think the Boys are really cool and they are very popular in England. Their concert in March was sold out within a couple of days of the tickets going on sale. I suppose one of the reasons I like BSB is because they are all themselves. They don't pretend to be anyone else or put on an act. They all seem like genuine, lovely people who must be really nice to be around.

Rachel Cohen
London, England

And here one dedicated BSB fan describes her view from the audience:

Rockin' with the Boys
by Jessica Horwood

My name is Jessica Horwood and I'm a huge BSB fan. I am fourteen years old. I have been a fan since the summer of 1996 when I first heard their song "We've Got It Goin' On" and saw a picture of the Backstreet Boys. I like their music because the fast songs are really upbeat and catchy, and being a dancer, I love to perform to them. Their slower ballads are very touching and deep—they speak straight to the heart.

I enjoy the Boys and their music so much that in March 1997 I created a Web site on the Internet about them called "Picke Bicke's Backstreet Boys Haven," which you can visit at http://www.geocities.com/Hollywood/Set/4023. Over four million fans of BSB have visited my site. A lot of people have told me that they find my site to be very informative and come to my page whenever they need to know something about the Backstreet Boys, such as lyrics to one of their songs. I love all of the Backstreet Boys very much, as do my three best friends, but if I had to pick my favorite one, I would choose A.J. Almost all of my friends are BSB fans, which I think is really cool.

Here is my own review of the Backstreet Boys concert at the Skydome in Toronto, Ontario, on January 3, 1998:

Approximately twenty-seven thousand screaming fans welcomed back the Backstreet Boys to

Toronto at the Skydome on January 3, 1998. The stadium had been sold out for this concert since late August 1997.

The fans that attended the concert were made up of mostly girls between the ages of eight and twenty-six, but also included the occasional guy and deafened parents who were there to keep an eye on their younger kids. The concert was roughly two hours long—not counting their opening act, Emjay, a solo artist, who was on for about a half hour or so to get the crowd pumped. I went to this concert with my three best friends, Laura Parker, Colleen Cater, and Mandy Emmerson.

During the concert, the Boys wore many different outfits. They started the concert wearing different-colored jogging suits: A.J. in blue, Brian in yellow, Howie in red, Kevin in black, and Nick in white. They opened the show with a huge *bang*. The first song was "That's The Way I Like It." It was followed by "I Wanna Be With You," during which Nick fell over while doing a dance step—the fall looked rehearsed, because he fell with legs flying in all directions. Next they all sang "Hey, Mr. DJ (Keep Playin' This Song)," but Howie disappeared near the end of the song to get ready for his solo.

The others left the stage as Howie appeared on a platform holding a bouquet of roses. He asked the crowd if they had had a happy new year, which led to screaming in response. He then started singing "Missing You." During the song, Howie gave out the roses to adoring fans. As he passed them out, the thought "Why couldn't that be me?" kept going through my mind. When he finished the song, an explosion of rose petals drifted down onto the audience.

A.J., whom I have a *mega* crush on, performed my favorite song, "Lay Down Beside Me," which made me cry. Kevin appeared next, singing "Nobody But You," and was followed by Brian singing and playing the song that he had written, titled "That's What She Said," during which he was hit on the butt by a teddy bear, which was thrown onstage by a fan. While standing on a platform, Nick sang the amazing yet sad song "Heaven In Your Eyes," bringing tears to everyone's eyes. The Boys performed their solos dressed in various white outfits, for example, A.J. was wearing a white long jacket, white pants, and a white baseball cap, with A.J. and Kevin baring buffed chests.

After the solos, the Boys remained on stage to sing "I'll Never Break Your Heart," followed by their newest single in Canada, "All I Have To Give." My friends and I were grooving throughout the whole concert. The Boys then sang and *played* "Quit Playing Games (With My Heart)," with Nick on drums, Kevin on keyboards, A.J. on bass, Howie on guitar, and Brian on the bongos. They sounded fantastic.

After they performed "Let's Have A Party," they sang "Anywhere For You," during which Brian brought out a beach ball like the one they had in the video for this song and threw the ball out into the crowd. After changing into black pants and black shirts, they performed "As Long As You Love Me," which was followed by the dance sequence with the chairs that was not featured in the video, which ended with them walking offstage to get ready for their encore.

For the encore, they came out wearing Canadian sports jerseys depicting the Blue Jays, the Argos, and the Maple Leafs. They sang three encore songs in all. First was "Get Down" and then they went straight into "We've Got It Goin' On."

Then they left the stage while bits of the "Everybody" video played on the four giant screens around the stage. A tall Grim Reaper appeared with glowing red eyes pushing a coffin (that I thought contained Howie). The Reaper then called forward four more Grim Reaper–like characters with the same glowing red eyes pushing four other coffins (which I thought was creepy). Fire blazed along the front and back of the stage as the coffins were turned around to reveal who was inside. The Boys were dressed in the costumes that they had worn for the last dance sequence of the "Everybody" video. Then they launched into the song "Everybody (Backstreet's Back)." It was truly amazing!

The choreography throughout the concert (some new to me and some I'd seen before) was fantastic. From all the hype they made about this concert, I think that it could be the next "live in concert" video.

Overall, I would say that this concert was *mega* compared to a previous Backstreet Boys concert that I attended on January 4, 1997, at the Warehouse in Toronto, Ontario. At that time, which was a year before I saw them at the Skydome, BSB weren't as popular as they are now, and although that concert was excellent, it didn't really compare to their 1998 show. Don't get me wrong, the Boys were still amazing, but I could really see how they've changed and improved over the year, performing new dance moves and trying out new things.

Fan Clubs

If you want to join one of the official fan clubs of the Backstreet Boys, you can! There is a U.S. fan club, as well as ones in Canada, Holland, and the United Kingdom. Each one costs a different amount and offers different BSB stuff, so contact the one you want to join to find out more. For the details, check out the BSB Resource Guide on pages 201–11 or go to the BSB official Web site at www.backstreetboys.com, which has the definitive scoop about the individual fan clubs and other official BSB info.

CHAPTER 13

Lover Boys

When it comes to getting to know and hanging out with ladies in a more than friendly way, the Boys simply don't have the time—or sometimes even the energy. Kevin jokes that usually he just goes to sleep early most nights. The Boys obviously come in constant contact with hundreds, even thousands of girls from all over the world. They see lots of girls in the audience with whom they think they could easily fall in love, they admit, but one meaningful look is certainly not enough to build an entire relationship on. The Boys might make the effort to try to spend some time talking with the fans with whom they feel a romantic connection, but they usually don't end up having a real opportunity to build any of these acquaintances and friendships into meaningful one-on-one relationships.

When asked which one of the Backstreet Boys is the most romantic with the ladies, they would all agree on A.J. He would win the award for Most Likely to Serenade Someone Special. He would also win for Biggest Flirt. Nick might be the runner-up. Brian might be voted Least Likely to Go Up to a Girl First, although you never know—the more girls they come in contact with as their popularity grows, the more comfortable they all might get with members of the opposite sex. But being a shy guy is not a bad thing, especially since plenty of girls like shy boys.

How to Know if a Backstreet Boy Is Flirting with You

Since they can rarely have full-fledged one-on-one relationships, the Boys have learned the fine art of flirting, so they can at least have some innocent fun with members of the opposite sex. Kevin said that when they were in Germany, they met some sexy dancers from Mr. President and Masterboy, so they spent some time flirting it up. But each of the Boys has his own unique style of flirting, depending on his personality. Here are some hints about each of the Boys' individual flirting techniques, in case you get lucky enough to need this kind of information.

What's Nick's secret flirting weapon? Eye contact. First, he looks at the girl until she looks back at him. If they hold each other's gaze, he takes that as a green light that it is okay to make a move. So he goes over to the girl and pays her compliments, perhaps about her hair or her eyes. Then they can start talking and getting to know each other. Later he might send her roses. What a romantic!

A.J. also goes for making eye contact, but he is a little less bold at first. He might pass by the girl a few times and just say hi before making any real move. Since A.J. is a natural conversationalist, most likely his big first move would be an intense conversation and lively storytelling. And if he really has a thing for a girl, he might launch into reciting some romantic poetry.

Kevin, even though he is the oldest, might be the shyest of the five. If he likes a girl, he will talk to her about topics of interest to him, like music or travel. It takes Kevin a long time to get comfortable enough to talk about his feelings right off, so the conversation will usually be about less personal topics.

Brian might be more the type who lets women come up to him. He is attracted to girls who are outgoing and independent, so if he liked someone, he might play it cool, sit back, and act a little hard to get. Brian is not into one-night stands and much prefers to take things slowly and steadily so that he can get to know a girl first.

When it comes to attracting members of the opposite sex, one never knows if Howie D. is going to turn on his "Sweet D." side and serenade a girl with a song, or his "Latin Lover" side and say something complimentary in Spanish. Either way, a girl who catches this BSBer's eye is in for a romantic time.

Figure Out Which Boy Is Best for You

You know what they look like. You know what they sound like. You know that they are good dancers. And by now (if you've been paying attention while you read this book) you probably know what kind of music they listen to, what they like to do in what little

free time they do have, what kind of clothes they like
to wear, and how many siblings each has.

But unless you have met your favorite BSBer personally and have spent some quality time with him,
you might not really know what he is looking for in a
girl and whether he is what you would be looking for
in a guy to spend time with in real life. So what's the
best way to find out which Backstreet Boy you would
be most compatible with? Consult the BSB Love Profiles below!

Love Profile of Nick

Since Nick was very young when he first became a
member of BSB, he used to be very shy when it came
to girls. None of the Boys had previously experienced
the kind of attention they now get from thousands of
female fans as BSBers, but Nick in particular hadn't
had a lot of experience with girls before setting out on
the road to stardom. In the beginning, he used to be
much shyer around girls, especially around someone
he liked. If he liked a person, he would get a tingly
feeling in his stomach and then not go near her.
Hardly the best way to win somebody's heart!

Nick hasn't yet been in love. As he gets a little older
he has begun to feel more comfortable around girls,
but he can still be shy when it comes to members of
the opposite sex. He seems to spend more time on the
basketball court or in front of his video games during
his free time than he does taking girls out on the town,
but that will probably be changing quite soon.

When Nick first started dating, he used to prefer brunettes with long hair, but now that he has a little more experience and a few more years under his belt, he doesn't have a preference. For Nick, what is inside is what counts—beauty on the outside isn't as important as beauty inside. When he thinks about what he prefers in a potential girlfriend, a good heart and a good personality top the list. Self-confidence is also appealing to him. He considers himself to be down-to-earth, so he would want to be with someone who would appreciate that about him. Since he believes he would be a loyal boyfriend, Nick wants to be with someone who is honest, too. If he ever finds that girl, she will be spoiled by an adoring Nick, who would be more than happy to treat his special someone right.

Turn-ons: Nick's dream girl shouldn't be shy. Instead, she should be full of self-confidence and know exactly what she is looking for and what she wants out of life. Nick describes this attitude as "sassy"—he likes a girl with sass.

Turn-offs: For Nick, the big no-no is lying and/or cheating. If someone isn't going to be up front with Nick, she probably shouldn't bother. And sorry, girls, smokers need not apply.

Dream date: Because the Boys' hectic schedule often puts the damper on having too many dates, Nick says that he tries to have fun and make the most of dates he does have.

Since Nick grew up not too far from the beach,

that's where he sees himself taking a girl for a special date: a moonlit walk down a beach with the calm water lapping softly at the shore. There would probably be more than one kind of star-gazing on that date.

Love Profile of Kevin

Kevin, the group's oldest member, is also probably the most old-fashioned of the crew when it comes to love, romance, and dating. If he is on a dinner date, he always opens the car door for a lady, pulls out her chair for her to sit down, and lets her order her food first. The royal treatment! He says his gentlemanly qualities come from the way his parents taught him to be: polite and respectful.

Ironically, even though Kevin is the oldest, he can sometimes be the shyest and most cautious when it comes to making the moves on girls. He knows how to flirt—and often does—but if he meets someone he thinks he might really like, he prefers to get to know her first as friends to see what interests they have in common before they get too deep.

Kevin is single right now but does do the dating thing. He doesn't think that going on one or two dates every so often is the same thing as having a relationship, but his schedule doesn't allow him time for much else. He thinks one important aspect of a relationship is spending a lot of quality time together, sharing thoughts, feelings, and experiences. He is old-fashioned and very romantic at heart. Kevin believes that when he meets the woman of his dreams, his soul mate, he will know it.

Turn-ons: Kevin does pay attention to a girl's clothes, and since he is a stylish dresser, he likes it when a girl wears funky, sexy clothes. Since Kevin was brought up to be a perfect gentleman, he would like to be with someone who has good manners as well. Personality-wise, Kevin's dream girl should be clever and smart.

Turn-offs: Kevin isn't looking for a girlfriend to be a servant to him. If a girl is not self-confident and doesn't pursue her own dreams, she is probably not the dream girl for him.

Dream date: Kevin's idea of a great date is pretty simple. It has to do more with the mood and feelings between him and his date than the atmosphere or activities. The food should be tasty and the conversation should be engaging. Good atmosphere and some dancing would be bonuses but are not crucial.

In the future, Kevin envisions himself being married and settled down with kids, which he is eager to have. Since Kevin has such a close family and lost his father not too long ago, he wants the opportunity to have a family of his own and be as good a father to his kids as his own father was to him and his siblings. But for the moment, BSB is Kevin's life—and he is putting most of his energies toward his work, which makes him very happy.

Love Profile of Howie D.

When it comes to dating and romance, Howie D.'s "Latin Lover" side comes out in full force. He is a die-hard sentimentalist who loves all the trappings of romance. Howie D. was anything but a late bloomer. He started romancing members of the fairer sex at a very young age.

Howie's first date was when he was only fourteen. The girl he asked out was in a play with him and was an "older woman" (only by a year, though), so her mother had to drive them. So much for a little privacy! Now that he is a bit older, he prefers more grown-up activities on his dates—and mothers are usually not invited. "Sweet D." also has a rep for being quite the romantic. He has written songs for girls and even sings to them during special moments. What girl wouldn't want a personal, one-on-one serenade from her favorite Backstreet Boy?

On the flip side, Howie is not really one to whisper sweet nothings in a girl's ear. He is a deep guy who only speaks from the heart. So if he doesn't have anything meaningful to say, he won't pretend that he does.

Always the perfect gentleman, Howie has never been slapped in the face by a girl (because he would never do anything that deserves such a response) nor has he ever cheated on a girlfriend. He admits to having a crush on more than one girl at a time, but two-timing is not in his vocabulary.

Unfortunately, as sweet as Howie is, he hasn't been able to duck getting his heart broken a couple of times. His past relationships have ended usually because the girl he was seeing can't really handle his intense traveling and touring schedule. He is rarely in one place—even home—for any substantial length of time, so that wears heavily on any kind of relationship he does get going. But just because that was the reason for his two biggest breakups, it didn't stop him from feeling the pain.

Turn-ons: Howie D. seems to know exactly what he is looking for in a girlfriend: someone who is spontaneous and doesn't care what others think of her for being so; someone whose sense of humor sparkles and who radiates self-confidence; someone who is warm and affectionate and generous with physical affection like hugs (which Howie loves); someone who is supportive of his work and career but who knows what she wants out of her life and goes for it; and someone who will fit in with his family and friends. Since he is so positive himself, it is important for the woman he is with to have a positive, optimistic outlook as well.

For the most part, a girl's looks are not the biggest deal to him, though he wouldn't mind meeting a blue-eyed girl, since he confesses he always wanted blue eyes. He wants someone who doesn't hide her real self by wearing things like big, baggy clothes or fake fingernails. His dream girl is someone who is comfortable with her femininity but who doesn't look or act like a precious doll. He likes people who aren't afraid to show who they really are—to him, that's very sexy. He is most attracted to women who have great charisma, but regardless of all of this, first and foremost his dream girl is someone with whom he can rap honestly and intimately.

Turn-offs: Howie gets turned off by arrogance. If a girl walks around like she is "all that," without concern for others, Howie is not interested. His family is very close and they all do things for one another. They share the household responsibilities, so no one gets more special treatment than another. His dream girl should be able to jump right into the way his family does things.

Dream date: Howie's idea of dream dates: maybe a surprise weekend trip, perhaps to a tropical beach; a romantic dinner, movies, and dancing, ending with a moonlight walk along the beach; or cooking a delicious dinner for his date at home. Howie would say that he has been told that he is a pretty decent kisser. He figures the more practice he gets, the better he will become!

Howie pictures himself married someday, but he is going to wait until he meets his dream girl.

Love Profile of Brian

For now, Brian seems to be happy doing his thing: being in BSB, being with his Boys, hanging out with Nick, playing basketball or video games. He does think about dating, and even though he is known for being the prankster of the group, he doesn't joke around when it comes to finding someone honest and true with whom he can connect in terms of values, both religious and moral, and interests.

Turn-ons: Brian is looking for someone who is smart—he won't compromise on intelligence—but at the same time, his special person needs to be someone who doesn't take life too seriously. She should possess a great sense of humor and lots of energy, matching his own. Brian also puts a nice and friendly personality at the top of his list. He also goes for girls with a natural look—not a lot of makeup, for instance. He'd be attracted to someone who can look great in jeans and who maybe has long hair, though it usually doesn't matter to him what color.

Turn-offs: Brian doesn't dig a girl who tries to tell him what to do. He does not like people who try to control other people. It bugs him when a fan tells him, "Take a picture with me now!"

Dream date: How would Brian plan a dream date? He would keep things simple, nothing too flashy, like a picnic in the park or a walk by a lake. The activity isn't as important to him as getting the opportunity to talk to his date and get to know her better.

Love Profile of A.J.

While seemingly the most confident and outgoing of the group, A.J. has been unlucky in love, which makes him a little more wary of jumping into romantic situations. His past experiences have ranged from downright tragic (a girl he dated when he was thirteen died in a car accident) to heartbreaking betrayals (he once found his girl kissing another guy).

That is not to say that with these less-than-fortunate experiences A.J. doesn't believe in love—he does. He still holds the hope that someday the perfect girl for him will cross his path. And how would that perfect girl be?

Turn-ons: A.J.'s idea of the perfect woman for him is someone who is sensitive but also has a sense of humor. She would have one side of her that is serious—intelligent and curious about the world, charismatic, and self-confident—and another side that is fun and light—humorous and with a weakness for junk food (if a girl can't enjoy scarfing down burgers and fries with A.J. at Mickey D's, she might not be the one for him). He would want this dream girl to be someone with whom he could share all of his thoughts and feelings. Self-confidence and independence are also major turn-ons for A.J.

Turn-offs: A.J. doesn't go for people who are dishonest.

Dream date: A.J. would be happy to accommodate a girl's preference for a dream date—he isn't particular about the activity. A.J. once went to a country line-dancing bar on a date, but if he needed to, he could plan a date filled with romance and fun. How about a roaring fire in the fireplace, mugs of hot chocolate with marshmallows, soft music, and mood lighting? Sounds like A.J. would know how to keep his date cozy and comfortable. He does say that a good date is one that ends warmly, with a soft kiss goodnight, a tight hug, and a handshake.

For the moment, though, A.J. is single and instead enjoys the friendship of many girls—perhaps more female friends than guy friends. He does make friends with some of his fans, too. He has been known to take the telephone numbers of some fans and surprise them later when he calls to meet up for breakfast.

Don't Lose Heart

The Boys all seem to be single right now. Many interviewers have asked the Boys several different times if they have girlfriends, and the answer always seems to be no. The guys are certainly flattered by all the attention they get from females, and most of them admit that they would date a fan if the feelings were there. The Boys do go out on dates when they get the chance, which unfortunately (in one respect) is not often, but that just means the Boys are out there playing for their fans and that BSB mania is still going strong. So you never know—you might turn out to be a BSBer's dream girl. . . .

CHAPTER 14

Crystal Ball

So far, the future seems very bright for the Backstreet Boys. They continue to grow in popularity as they win the hearts of fans all over the world with their hot sounds, sexy dance moves, handsome looks, and fan-pleasing performances. They show no signs of slowing down—their current schedule keeps them booked with gigs and appearances months in advance, not only in the United States and Canada, but all over the world, wherever fans are keeping Backstreet pride alive. It seems that as long as the group keeps turning out the hit singles, the Boys will make the rounds, givin' their fans their all.

What are their plans for the future—individually and as a group?

Is Another Album in the Works?

The Boys have headed back to Sweden to start recording their second U.S. album. They might include some of the songs that were used on their second internationally released CD and record some new songs to finish out the mix. They plan to work with some of the producers with whom they have already worked, since they proved to be such great teams before. They also have some songs that weren't able to be finished in time for their first U.S. release, so they plan to get back to those, refining them so they can be included on the new CD.

Will They Keep It Together?

In an live interactive interview with BSB on America Online in October 1997, the Boys were asked how long they plan to continue to sing together as a group. Howie's response was "as long as you love me," which brought a lot of "awww's" from the other Boys.

Seriously though, for the time being, all of them seem to plan on being together long into the future. The five of them *are* the Backstreet Boys—a team, a family—so if one of the Boys wanted out, they would have to decide as a group whether to replace that person or disband entirely. So far, that is not happening.

A few of them speak of trying their hands at solo singing careers, but they would plan to stay with the group while they were pursuing their own things. They use the example set by New Edition, one of their boy band predecessors, as the optimal way a group should handle their individual and joint careers. New Edition first became known as a group in the 1980s, then went off to do solo projects in the late 1980s and early 1990s, and then got together again in the late '90s, with their added new experiences, to produce new hits.

But all of the Boys agree that doing something on their own is far off down the road. For now, they are thrilled to be together doing what they love most.

What Dreams Do the Boys Have for the Future?

Brian and Kevin, the Kentucky cousins, share the desire to get married someday and have big families—really settle down and relax. Kevin adds that perhaps he would try returning to acting. In ten years, Kevin hopes, he will be starting a family, something to which he wants to devote himself fully when the time comes.

Nick actually has a theatrical agent in case he decides to return to acting—but there are no firm plans for that yet. Since one of Nick's passions is basketball and he spends so much of what little free time he has playing, in the future he would want to get really good at it, perhaps even go to a college and play for their team. If he did go to college, Nick might want to major in Art, since he loves to draw so much. At the moment Nick calls his parents' house his home and says he plans to continue living with them for the foreseeable future.

Howie sees music in his future for a long time. But he also wants to add acting and more dancing into the mix. He loves performing and entertaining, so he would want all of that to be a part of his future.

A.J. also has several goals in music that he wants to achieve in the not-too-distant future. For instance, he would love to perform on the MTV Music Awards in the States. A.J. also wants to perform with the group No Doubt—not only because he likes their sound, but also because he is harboring a big-time crush on their beautiful blond lead singer, Gwen Stefani. He still envisions the Boys together in ten years, but by that point in their career, he sees them having much more creative control and being more involved in the production and stage show. A.J. would also like to write music someday—for himself as well as other artists.

All of the Boys seem to want to do more song-writing and become increasingly more involved in the group's creative process and planning. Since many of them have backgrounds in acting, there have been some offers made to the Boys, but it doesn't seem that the Boys will have much time to follow up on them anytime soon.

What's the Word on the Street?

There is word that a Backstreet Boys movie is in the works and that they want it to have a gothic-comic-book-like feel, based on the comic books that Nick is working on. Someday Nick wouldn't mind publishing a Backstreet Boys comic book, too, if he can come up with the right story. But so far there have been no confirmations of any film-related plans or official word about a book illustrated by Nick. For the moment, fans

will have to be satisfied with their concert video and
seeing their favorite Boys appear on TV.

Whom Would the Boys Like to Work with Next if They Could Choose?

R. Kelly is one of their top choices. They would like
to do some duets with female artists at some point,
such as Robyn, who is from Sweden and who has the
hit "Show Me Love." Since they have done some pre-
liminary work with one of their idols, Babyface, they
would like to have the opportunity to continue their
work with him in the near future.

Will Any of the Boys' Siblings Get into the Act?

Yes, but his own. There seems to be a bright future
in entertainment for one of the Boys' sibs: Nick's little
brother, Aaron Carter—who turned ten years old on
December 7, 1997, and has a twin sister, Angel, who
is one minute older—has his own hit single! Little
Aaron released a single called "Crush On You," on
August 18, 1997, in fourteen foreign countries,
including Germany, Austria, Switzerland, France, Italy,
Spain, and the Netherlands. The video for the song is
already in rotation on Much Music. In the fall of 1997
Nick's little brother joined BSB on tour to perform his
hit single. If Aaron is anything like his big bro, Nick,
then you'd better watch out for him to follow in his
brother's *very large and famous* footsteps!

What Do the Stars Say About
Each of the Boys' Futures?

To answer this question, I turned to Andrea Valeria,
who is a well-known astrologer and author in the
United States and Mexico. Her newest book, *Illumi-
nated Choices: The Essential Handbook for Making
Astrologically Informed Decisions*, is going to be published in early 1999. She looked at the stars to see
what they hold in store for A.J., Nick, Kevin, Brian,
and Howie D. in the near future.

The number of days between the birth of Nick (the
youngest member in BSB) and Kevin (the oldest) is
3,039. In numerology, this might just be a magic
number if you add 3+0+3+9 (never underestimate
the power of a zero!), which equals 15. Then, add 1 to
5, which equals 6. Six is a lucky number for all the
Boys to have because six is the number that signifies
perfection. It also is the number that connects human
beings to the cosmos, which means that BSB has the
stars on their side!

Astrological Profile for Kevin—Libra

During all those days between Kevin and Nick's
births, there were 101 full moons, which gives Kevin
almost an overdose of feelings, because of his versa-
tile and sensitive moon sign, which is Pisces. Maybe,
just maybe, he is the wisest of the five Boys. His moon
sign in Pisces, combined with his sun sign in Libra,
makes him a person who ponders and weighs all of his

actions before he does them. This combination also
makes Kevin a "funnel of sensitivity," meaning that
he can channel all of the emotions he stirs in other
people—just by being around them—and draw energy
from them. Kevin is probably much nicer than he himself would like to admit—he sure can turn on the
charm when he finds it convenient to do so. This next
year should get better and better for him in all areas of
his life.

Astrological Profile for Howie D.—Leo

Howie could bully all his listeners into not wanting
to hear anything else but *his* music. He is, after all, a
Leo, and Leos know how to get others to do anything
they want! Howie and Nick might just team up and
start writing some poetry together, because they both
have their moon signs in Gemini, which means both of
them have a close connection to words. (By the way,
the moon sign, which everyone has no matter when
you were born, is also considered the part of your
astrological profile that is the "love promoter.")
Howie D. might convince himself that he is slightly
fickle, but this year someone or something will definitely put him in his rightful place, which is as the
head of something—a relationship, an entity, or a
movement of some kind. He could use his fast-talking
charm to get what he wants out of life, as long as he is
careful not to talk himself into getting involved with
something controversial. But even if he does flirt with
controversy, he probably will come out a winner!

Astrological Profile of Brian—
Aquarius on the Cusp of Pisces

Brian was born on a day when the sun actually changed signs from Aquarius to Pisces. Because he was born during such a time, Brian carries the force of change in his chart. He has the capability of changing people's lives or emotions with a wink of his eye or a killer smile. Brian was set on earth as a Pisces with reserve and a rather cool, refined (if he would put his mind to it—or wanted it, for that matter), and quirky sense of humor. This year should be great fun for him if he doesn't let his heart get in his way. He may think he is a loner, but the loner of the group is actually A.J.

Astrological Profile of A.J.—Capricorn

A.J. is a double Capricorn, meaning he has both his sun and moon signs in Capricorn. If that double dose doesn't help him fatten his bank account this year, he will be doing himself a double disfavor, because the stars indicate lots of cash in the drawer! Adoring fans can sigh about him all they want, but you can be sure that the girl who can get through to his core is in for a kind of substantial advantage (and I'm not talking money-wise). Whoever this girl is, she'd better plan on being in it with A.J. for the long haul, which is how long any plans with A.J. should last. A.J. could be a good leader if he dared to be one. A.J. can also be crafty when it comes to concealing his moods, and he might hold a grudge longer than any of the other

Boys. But then again, there is always a purpose behind his actions, and this year his actions will put him at the top!

Astrological Profile of Nick—Aquarius

Nick's sign makes him the transformer of the group. When he puts his mind to it, he can be a major catalyst for bringing about change or new situations. Nick is much more resourceful than he seems, which means that when he doesn't get his way the first time around, he just waits for the second time. If he keeps a diary, it would be the best thing that ever could be read out loud at a party, especially if he has written down what actually happened as well as what he really would have liked to have happen because for Nick, there is a thin line between reality (how everyone else sees it) and the way Nick sees reality. (That's probably why Nick is so good at drawing cartoons and comics!) Sometimes he can scare himself, especially when things work out just as he thought they would. So this year he should try thinking positively and feeling those thoughts deep down inside—maybe even try some meditation, which would help him find out more about his true inner self. Nick's combination of an Aquarius sun sign and a Gemini moon can at times be dynamite!

BSB Resource Guide

Here's your guide for where to find, access, buy, see, experience, and enjoy all things Backstreet!

Official Backstreet Boys Web Site

Check out www.backstreetboys.com for the latest news, schedule and tour information, member bios, video and audio clips, press releases, charity info, etc. about the Boys. Also includes information about joining the premium on-line service "Backstreet Boys V.I.P."

Or write:

"Backstreet Boys V.I.P."
c/o Carlson Sterling Inc.
P.O. Box 691658
Orlando, FL 32869-1658

Official Fan Club Info

If you want to join one of the official fan clubs of the Backstreet Boys, you can! There is a U.S. fan club, as well as ones in Canada, the Netherlands, and the United Kingdom. Each one costs a different amount and offers different BSB stuff, so contact the one you want to join to find out more. The BSB official Web site at www.backstreetboys.com has the scoop about the individual fan clubs.

The info:

The U.S.A. Backstreet Boys Fan Club:
Fan Club Membership
Backstreet Boys
P.O. Box 618203
Orlando, FL 32861-8203
(as of December 1997, membership cost is $19.95)
Toll-free number:
1-888-344-7717

The Canadian Backstreet Boys Fan Club:
Backstreet Boys
Canadian Fan Club
Suite 1231
1930 Yonge Street
Toronto, Ontario
M4S 1Z7
Canada
(as of December 1997, membership is Cdn $27.95)

The Netherlands Backstreet Boys Fan Club:
Fan Club Membership
Backstreet Boys
P.O. Box 713
4116ZJ Buren (Gld)
The Netherlands

The U.K. Backstreet Boys Fan Club:
Fan Club Membership
Backstreet Boys Fan Club
P.O. Box 20
Manchester M60 3ED
United Kingdom

Backstreet Boys Official Fan Merchandise

T-shirts, sweatshirts, throw pillows, bandannas, keychains, baseball caps, posters, and the Backstreet Boys videos *Backstreet Boys: The Video* and *Backstreet Boys Live in Concert*—catalog can be found both on their official Web site and in their U.S.-released CD *Backstreet Boys*. To order, call toll free: 1-800-694-1334

Discography

Backstreet Boys—American release, release date August 12, 1997, from Trans Continental/Jive Records

"We've Got It Goin' On"
"Quit Playing Games (With My Heart)" (extended version)
"As Long As You Love Me"
"All I Have To Give"
"Anywhere For You"
"Hey, Mr. DJ (Keep Playin' This Song)"
"I'll Never Break Your Heart"
"Darlin' "
"Get Down (You're The One For Me)"
"Set Adrift On Memory Bliss"
"If You Want It To Be Good Girl (Get Yourself A Bad Boy)"

Enhanced CD version includes: biography of the Backstreet Boys, including individual profiles of the group members; video clips for "Quit Playing Games (With My Heart)" and "We've Got It Goin' On"; "Hangin' With The Boys" section featuring the Boys telling all kinds of fun facts about themselves, their tours, and their music; "Cool Stuff," with info about BSB official merchandise, such as videos and CDs, and Web site address; and a BSB quiz—if you answer it correctly, you get to see a bonus video clip of BSB singing "Anywhere For You" live on VIVA television in Germany. (Use this book to find the answers to the quiz questions!)

Backstreet Boys—first European release, U.K. release date September 1996

  "We've Got It Goin' On"
  "Anywhere For You"
  "Get Down (You're The One For Me)"
  "I'll Never Break Your Heart"
  "Quit Playing Games (With My Heart)"
  "Boys Will Be Boys"
  "Just To Be Close To You"
  "I Wanna Be With You"
  "Every Time I Close My Eyes"
  "Darlin' "
  "Let's Have A Party"

Backstreet Boys—first Canadian release, release date September 1996

  "We've Got It Goin' On"
  "Get Down (You're The One For Me)"

"I'll Never Break Your Heart"
"Quit Playing Games (With My Heart)"
"Boys Will Be Boys"
"Just To Be Close To You"
"I Wanna Be With You"
"Every Time I Close My Eyes"
"Darlin' "
"Roll With It"

Backstreet's Back—second European release, release date August 1997

"Everybody (Backstreet's Back)"
"As Long As You Love Me"
"All I Have To Give"
"That's The Way I Like It"
"10,000 Promises"
"Like A Child"
"Hey, Mr. DJ (Keep Playin' This Song)"
"Set Adrift On Memory Bliss"
"That's What She Said"
"If You Want It To Be Good Girl (Get Yourself A Bad Boy)"
"If I Don't Have You"

Backstreet's Back—second Canadian release, release date August 1997

"Everybody (Backstreet's Back)"
"As Long As You Love Me"
"All I Have To Give"
"That's The Way I Like It"

"10,000 Promises"

"Like A Child"

"Hey, Mr. DJ (Keep Playin' This Song)"

"Set Adrift On Memory Bliss"

"That's What She Said"

"Anywhere For You"

"If You Want It To Be Good Girl (Get Yourself A
    Bad Boy)"

"If I Don't Have You"

Other Books About the Backstreet Boys

The Backstreet Boys, by K. S. Rodriguez (Harper
    Active, a division of HarperCollins Publishers,
    1997), $4.99. ISBN: 0-06-107075-0. 128 pages
    with 8-page black-and-white photo insert. For
    younger readers; was written before the Boys hit it
    big in the States.

Backstreet Boys: From Florida with Love! (Omnibus
    Press, 1997), $9.95. ISBN: 0-7119-6574-9. 32
    pages, full-color photos throughout. Mostly pictures
    with some text, mostly about the group's success in
    the United Kingdom and Europe in 1995 and 1996.

Soon to be published: *The Making of "Backstreet's
    Back,"* by Denise McLean (A.J.'s mother!). 52 pages,
    limited edition illustrated book. Will take you on a
    behind-the-scenes walk through the making of the
    video "Everybody (Backstreet's Back)." See the offi-
    cial Backstreet Boys Web site for more information.

U.S. Magazines to Check Out That Regularly Feature
the Backstreet Boys

Tiger Beat: Available at most bookstores and
   newsstands, or go to http://www.nextlevel.com/
   tigerbeat for ordering info, or write to Sterling/
   MacFadden, 35 Wilbur Street, Lynbrook, NY 11563.

BB: Available at most bookstores and newsstands.

Teen: Available at most bookstores and newsstands.

Teen Beat: Available at most bookstores and
   newsstands.

16:   Available at most bookstores and newsstands.

Unofficial Backstreet Boys Web Sites

Most things on the Web constantly change—sites
come and go, URLs change, one day you can find a
site, another day you can't. So while there seem to be
dozens of unofficial Web sites dedicated to BSB
hosted by fans all over the world in several different
languages, I've only listed some of the better sites that
seem to have been around the longest thus far, are
among the least faulty/buggy, and are updated on a
somewhat regular basis. These sites have no official
connection with the Backstreet Boys or any of the
companies with which BSB are associated, so don't

necessarily take everything you read and see on these sites as the absolute truth. Also, even though I have tried to be selective, some of the listings below might not be up and running on the Web when you go to check them out, so apologies in advance.

A couple of other words of caution: (1) Beware of computer viruses, especially if you are trying to download stuff from the Web onto your hard drive. Some of the less-than-reputable sites contain nasty viruses, which are a pain to get rid of and can possibly damage your hardware—so exercise caution and be sure you have some kind of virus protection program that scans the files you want to download. (2) If you are under eighteen years old, you might want to check with your parents or guardian before purchasing goods or services or before giving out personal information over the Net on these unofficial sites.

Besides visiting the sites listed below, you can also conduct your own Web search by using any of the Web search engines found on your Internet browser or the home pages of your ISP, such as Yahoo!, Excite, InfoSeek, Web Crawler, etc., by typing in "Backstreet Boys" as your key words. Geocities hosts a lot of these unofficial sites, so you could visit their home page, www.geocities.com, and look under their entertainment and music categories to find sites that might not have listings with the major search engines. You might also want to check out the "Bubblegum Music" pages of the Mining Company (www.miningco.com) at http://bubblegummusic.miningco.com, which has some cool stuff about the Backstreet Boys and other popular boy bands such as Boyzone and Hanson.

Many of the unofficial BSB-related sites below and the ones you will find through the search engines are connected by Web rings or something called the BSB Internet Alliance—again, unofficial entities—which means that many of the hosts of these unofficial Web sites have joined together to help promote one another's sites. The good thing for you is that once you arrive at a site that is a member of one of these groups, you can usually find links to a bunch of other related sites.

Happy surfing!

Picke Bicke's BSB Haven: www.geocities.com/Hollywood/Set/4023. Hosted by our very own guest contributor to Chapter 12, Jessica Horwood. Full of hot news, pics, song lyrics, and a chat forum, among other great features. Stop by and say hi to Jessica!

Jill's Backstreet Boys Heaven: www.execulink.com/~wmgp/Default.htm. Includes a great feature called "Fan of the Week," fan survey, chat, and news.

Backstreet Boys on the Net: www.geocities.com/SunsetStrip/Palms/4622. Winner of the Starting Point Hot Site Award. Includes member bios, scrapbook full of magazine articles about the Boys, articles written by BSB fans, lyrics, BSB astrology, links, surveys, and debates.

The Singapore Backstreet Boys Homepage: www.
geocities.com/SunsetStrip/Towers/3717. Includes
the latest scoops about BSB, a photo gallery, FAQs,
articles, concert and CD reviews, links, a swap
shop, and a useful archive of past articles about
the Boys.

The Mariah Carey–Backstreet Boys R&B Web Page:
www.geocities.com/RainForest/5882. Despite its
double fan focus, this is a great site for BSB stuff
and has all kinds of creative pages, such as the BSB
Tax Audit, which helps you determine how much
money you spend on your BSB obsession; also has
a feedback forum, goofs and gaffs, and real-time
chat. Is the twin site of Backstreet Online, below,
and shares the same exhaustive, excellent link list
with the Backstreet Boys Internet Fan Club, also
listed below.

Backstreet Online: www.rogerswave.ca/kwan. This
Canadian-based site is a member of the BSB
Internet Alliance, seems to be updated regularly,
and is one of the better sites. Includes the BSB tour
and TV appearance schedule (for Canada mostly),
Boys bloopers, pen pals, and a great list of links.

The Backstreet Boys Internet Fan Club: www.geocities.
SunsetStrip/Palms/7002. Offers high- and low-tech
viewing options to accommodate different browser
versions; also has French and Canadian versions of
the site; has an unofficial fan club.

Tanya's Backstreet Boys: www.angelfire.com/TANYABSB/.
Includes interviews, member bios, swap-and-sell
page, pictures, and a scrawl wall.

To get the latest music chart information from
around the world, you can also check out the following sites (which often have links to other charts):

Billboard magazine (United States): www.billboard-
online.com
MTV Australia: www.village.com.au/mtv
Much Music (the music video channel in Canada):
www.chumcity.com/muchmusic/

GOLDEN BOY
The Matt Damon Story

by Kristen Busch

Golden Globe and Academy Award winner Matt Damon's meteoric rise to superstardom is the stuff of Hollywood legend. Only one year ago, hardly anyone had heard of Damon, despite an impressive list of film credits that included pivotal roles in *School Ties, Courage Under Fire,* and *The Rainmaker.* But with the release of *Good Will Hunting,* which he cowrote and costarred in with best friend Ben Affleck, Matt is everywhere.

And GOLDEN BOY tells the whole story: from his modest beginnings through his college years at Harvard and beyond to writing, selling, and starring in his own screenplay. It seems the sky is the limit for Damon—who has been linked with some of Hollywood's most beautiful young actresses! This is an insightful look at the life of this brilliant young writer, actor, and Academy Award winner.

Published by Ballantine Books.
Available wherever books are sold.

Coming in June '98

HEART SONG
The Story of Jewel

by Scott Gray

Since the release of her debut CD, *Pieces of You*, soulful singer/songwriter Jewel Kilcher has blossomed into, perhaps, the most popular woman in today's music scene. Jewel has touched the world with raw honesty and a voice as beautifully expansive as her native Alaska landscape.

Here are the intriguing details and little-known facts of her life. From a childhood spent on a rustic homestead to her struggle to overcome dyslexia through weekly gigs at a San Diego coffeehouse and her breakthrough to superstardom, HEART SONG journeys to the core of this original and insightful poet/musician.

Published by Ballantine Books
Available soon wherever books are sold